FOOLPROOF ITALIAN COOKERY

ALDO ZILLI

FOOLPROOF ITALIAN COOKERY

ALDO ZILLI

Step by step to
everyone's favourite
Italian recipes

Acknowledgements

First I would like to thank you for buying my book, and I hope you will get as much pleasure from recreating my recipes as I did writing them.

After my third book I said to my lovely agent, Fiona Lindsay, please don't get me any more book deals because of the time and effort it takes, but she convinced me that it would get easier and easier. So I agreed to do this one and I am really pleased I did, because I enjoyed writing it much more than the others.

A very special thank you goes to a very special person, my personal assistant, Luisa Alves, for working wonders with all my scribbles. What would I do without her?

Another special thank you goes to my home economist, Suzy Theodora, who always blames me for making her put on weight, as she has to test all the recipes.

A big *grazie* goes to Enzo di Marino, my head chef, who helped me to create some of the best recipes. As we both come from the same region in Italy we understand each other really well … so important when you share a kitchen with someone, especially when it gets very hot!

A big thank you to my family too for putting up with me.

Food photography by Jean Cazals

Published by BBC Worldwide Ltd,
Woodlands, 80 Wood Lane,
London W12 0TT

First published 2001
Copyright © Aldo Zilli 2001
The moral right of the author has been asserted.

Food photography © Jean Cazals 2001

ISBN 0 563 55196 8

Commissioning editor: Vivien Bowler
Project editor: Helena Caldon
Copy-editor: Jane Middleton
Art direction: Lisa Pettibone
Designer: Susannah Good
Home economist: Marie Ange Lapierre
Stylist: Sue Rowlands

The publishers would like to thank David Mellor for supplying items used in the photographs

Set in Univers
Printed and bound in Singapore by Tien Wah Press
Colour separations by Kestrel Digital Colour, Chelmsford
Printed paper case and jacket by Tien Wah Press

Contents

Introduction

When I was a boy, money was always tight, as I was the youngest of eight children. My mother had to make do with whatever was available in the garden. Luckily we had a large garden, so we could grow all the vegetables and herbs we needed. We lived near the sea and during the school holidays I would help the local fishermen, who paid me in fish. So in summer, fish was always on the menu, cooked in a variety of ways with our garden produce and pasta or gnocchi.

From a very young age, I loved helping my mum in the kitchen. She used to create the best dishes with just a few fresh ingredients and a passion that characterizes Italian food all over the world. So please don't be worried about cooking any of my recipes. If you are short of an ingredient, don't panic; just substitute or do without and you can create your own dishes.

Italian chefs are naturals in the kitchen because from an early age the family tradition of cooking and eating together creates a passion for food, and life in general.

Through this book I hope I can share some of my passion for Italian food. So get cooking these great but simple dishes!

Over the last 20 years, I have cooked certain recipes over and over again, in various restaurants and in my own home. So I thought I would share some of my family favourites with you in this book, such as Tagliatelle Carbonara, Rigatoni with Traditional Pork Bolognese and Pork Valdostana. This book shows how easy Italian cooking is, especially since it has become one of the world's most popular cuisines. Nowadays even English cooks enjoy preparing Italian food, as we can see with Jamie Oliver and Delia Smith, two of my favourite television chefs. Part of the attraction of Italian cooking is the simplicity of the ingredients, most of which are easy to find now that supermarkets stock a large selection of fresh and dried Italian produce. However, it is always a good idea to visit an Italian deli for your essentials, such as good pasta, olives, Parmesan cheese, and Pavesini biscuits to make your tiramisu much lighter.

Remember, cooking is supposed to be fun, so get in your kitchen and enjoy yourself – and don't forget to include the kids, so they can grow up without being scared of cooking and learn to love food, like I did.

Ingredients and Equipment

INGREDIENTS

Italian food is renowned for its freshness and flavour. This section lists some of the more mainstream Italian ingredients and will give you a helping hand when you are doing your food shopping.

Anchovies

These tiny fish are available either preserved in salt or oil. The ones packed in salt are the best, and you should be able to find them in Italian delicatessens, in tins or sold by weight. They need a good wash and soaking in water before use to remove as much of the salt as possible. In most recipes you can substitute anchovy fillets in oil if you can't get the salted ones.

Clockwise from top left: borlotti beans, cannellini beans, salted capers, balsamic vinegar

Balsamic vinegar

This mahogany-coloured vinegar from Modena has a syrupy consistency and is low in acidity. It is aged in wooden barrels over many years, with the type of wood and size of barrel changing each year to produce a complex, concentrated flavour. It is primarily used uncooked, either in dressings or drizzled on cheese or fruit.

The best balsamic vinegars may be aged for as long as 50 years and are very expensive. If you are using a cheap balsamic vinegar, a good trick to enrich its flavour is to boil it until reduced by half, then mix it with oil as usual to make a dressing.

Beans

Italians use a lot of dried beans in soups and stews, such as borlotti, cannellini and chickpeas. However, there is such a good range of tinned beans available now that it hardly seems worth having to soak dried beans overnight and boiling them for hours on end. If you use canned beans, drain them well and rinse them under cold running water before use. However, don't forget fresh borlotti or cannellini beans in season. Once shelled, these do not take very long to cook and their flavours are fabulous.

Capers

Capers are the small flower buds of a Sicilian bush that grows near the coast. They are preserved in salt or vinegar and are used to flavour salads, fish dishes and various antipasti. Be sure to rinse them well before use. I prefer small capers, which have a better flavour and are more tender.

Cheese
Fontina
This is a semi-soft cow's milk cheese with a delicate, nutty, almost honeyed flavour. It is used extensively in northern Italian cooking.

Mascarpone

Mascarpone is a very rich cream cheese from Lombardy, commonly used in desserts or pasta sauces. The colour can vary from snow white to straw yellow.

Mozzarella

Most mozzarella is made from cow's milk. It is porcelain white and springy in texture, with a milky aftertaste. Buffalo mozzarella is made from buffalo's milk and is far superior in flavour and texture. Always buy mozzarella in milky water (sold either loose or in little bags) and store it in the water, otherwise it will harden and the flavour will become bitter.

Parmesan

The best Parmesan is parmigiano reggiano, the finest of all Italian grating cheeses. Like extra virgin olive oil and balsamic vinegar, it is expensive but well worth the price. A piece of parmigiano, wrapped in waxed paper and then in foil, will keep for months in the refrigerator. Besides being used in cooking, it is delicious served with fruit, especially ripe pears and figs. Don't bother buying pre-grated Parmesan cheese, unless it is freshly grated from a good Italian deli.

Try not to add Parmesan to every pasta dish or they will start to taste the same. (Having said this, I love it with everything and even sometimes break the rule that it should not be teamed with seafood.) It is particularly good with porcini mushrooms or spicy sauces.

Pecorino

There are several versions of this sheep's milk cheese available, varying according to where they have been produced and whether they have been aged. For grating, choose pecorino romano, a hard cheese with a slightly oily texture and a sharp, salty taste. Fresh pecorino cheese, from Tuscany or Sardinia, is too soft for grating and has a very different flavour.

Ricotta

This soft, fresh sheep's milk cheese is one of the most versatile cheeses to come out of my country. I love it with pasta (try adding it to the cherry tomato sauce on page 48), risotto (marvellous served with Pumpkin and Jumbo Prawn Risotto, page 68), in stuffings (Roasted Stuffed Onions, page 42) and, of course, as a

Clockwise from top left: Parmesan, mozzarella, mascarpone, ricotta

dessert (Ricotta and Amarena Cherry Tart, page 110). It also tastes fabulous by itself with fruit, particularly if you can find fresh ricotta rather than the sort sold in tubs. If you are lucky enough to have access to a good Italian deli, seek out ricotta salata. This is a firmer cheese that has been salted, making its texture more like that of the Greek feta. It is very good served with ripe tomatoes and crusty bread.

Chillies

Dried chilli flakes are excellent in tomato sauces, since they give them a lift but are not hot enough to burn. I like adding long, red, fairly mild fresh chillies to marinades for meat, fish and shellfish that are going to be cooked quickly. When using fresh chillies it's up to you how much you add; if you want a milder flavour, remove and discard the seeds and membranes, which carry most of the capsaicin, the source of the chilli's heat.

In Abruzzo, where I grew up, and Molise, extra virgin olive oil is infused with chillies for a week and then used on meat, fish, grains and salads. It is quite a powerful condiment and not for the fainthearted.

Cured meats
Bresaola
Bresaola is cured beef that has been salted, marinated and then air-dried. It comes from the Valtellina region to the north-east of Milan, which is famous for its beef. When sliced, it has a deep ruby-red colour and sweet, aromatic flavour. For an extremely simple starter or a nibble to serve with drinks, arrange several wafer-thin slices of bresaola on a flat plate, overlapping slightly, and dress it with freshly squeezed lemon juice, extra virgin olive oil and some freshly ground black pepper. Serve with grissini.

Pancetta
This is Italian unsmoked bacon, cured with salt and spices. It has a good strong flavour which means that a small piece will go a long way. It will keep for weeks either hanging in a cool, dry place or in the refrigerator. Try it finely diced in tomato sauces or added to dried beans as they cook so that the flavour will penetrate the beans. If you do not have any pancetta, you can try using unsmoked bacon in its place. There is a classic pasta

sauce made with pancetta which is Carbonara (see page 58).

Prosciutto
Prosciutto is a type of cured ham made from year-old pigs, which are raised on a special diet of whey left over from cheese making. It is dark pink in colour with ribbons of fat. Parma ham is a type of prosciutto made near Parma, for which the pigs are raised traditionally and fed on the whey from parmigiano reggiano cheese. It is believed by many to be the most luxurious of all cured meats, although this is disputed by those who prefer prosciutto from San Daniele and Sauris in the region of Friuli. They are all full of flavour, whether served alone as an antipasto or starter, or used to give extra oomph to chicken, pork or steak.

Garlic
There are now several varieties of garlic available. The summer sees the arrival of large bulbs of juicy, fresh garlic, which is brilliant roasted whole with game. Elephant garlic, which is much larger than ordinary garlic, is quite mild and needs to be used quickly as it tends to dry out. The small heads of purple garlic are milder and juicier than white, papery ones.

Buy firm bulbs of garlic and store them in a cool, dry place, but not the refrigerator. It will keep for several weeks. Old garlic often has a green sprout in the centre of each clove, which should be removed before use because of its bitter taste. Do not substitute dried or powdered garlic for fresh.

When cooking garlic, sauté it gently in oil or butter without colouring; browning will make it bitter. I prefer to crush each clove and then remove when serving the sauce, so that no one gets a mouthful of garlic.

Herbs
Basil
This is the herb most closely associated with Italian cooking. With its sweet flavour and aroma, it is the perfect partner for tomatoes and is also used in large quantities to make pesto. Always use fresh rather than dried basil. The pots now widely available in supermarkets are ideal for Italian cooking; keep them on a sunny windowsill and they will thrive for up to a month. Red, or purple,

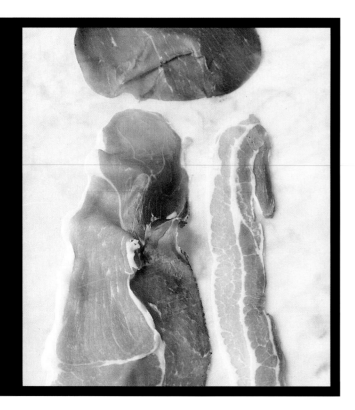

Clockwise from top: bresaola, pancetta, prosciutto

basil has a very similar flavour to green but makes an interesting visual change for salads, garnishes and pesto.

Oregano
Oregano has a slightly sweet flavour but is not as fragrant as basil. It is excellent with meats, cheeses and vegetables, especially tomatoes, potatoes and courgettes. Try sautéeing courgettes with oregano and serve with a couple of fried eggs – a perfect quick lunch or supper.

Parsley
The flat-leaf variety, which I also call Italian parsley, has a stronger flavour than the English curly parsley and looks more attractive too. The flat-leaf parsley sold in pots is rather weak in flavour and flimsy to work with, so try to find hardier bunches, with thick green stems and deep green leaves, available in some supermarkets and all good ethnic greengrocers'. Use flat-leaf parsley in tomato sauces or simply to dress barbecued or grilled fish, along with lemon juice and extra virgin olive oil.

Rosemary
This pungent, earthy herb with savoury aromas is the perfect partner for lamb. However, it is also very good with pork and strong-flavoured fish such as monkfish, prawns and salmon. If using dried rosemary, you will only need a quarter of the required quantity of fresh. Rosemary can be easily dried in the sunlight and then crumbled off the stems and stored in an airtight jar. Use the thick, woodier stalks as skewers for kebabs: remove the leaves, leaving some at the top end, and pierce through vegetables, fish or meat; the food will be infused with the flavour of rosemary as it cooks.

Sage
This herb should always be served cooked. Its strong, musty flavour works well in one of the easiest pasta sauces: simply fry sage leaves in butter, then pour them over plain cooked pasta or ravioli. Sage is also good with meat and well-flavoured fish and shellfish.

Mushrooms
Field mushrooms
These large, flat mushrooms (sometimes called portabello) are more likely to be

Clockwise from top left: basil, oregano, sage, flat-leaf parsley, rosemary

cultivated than wild nowadays but they are still full of good flavour. Smaller flat field mushrooms (portabellini) are also available. However, it is wild mushrooms that Italians go crazy about. They have an intense flavour and a few go a long way when mixed with flat field mushrooms.

Chanterelles
These are either golden or reddish-orange, with a firm texture and a solid shape that looks as if it should be floppy! Their mild flavour is ideal for sautés, as they soak up the flavours of garlic, butter and fresh herbs. Look out for them in summer and autumn.

Morels
These highly prized mushrooms look rather different from the classic mushroom shape, with a pitted, honeycomb-like cap sitting on a hollow stem. Available in spring and early summer, they have an affinity with cream-based sauces. They need thorough cleaning before use as they can harbour insects and grit.

Clockwise from top: field mushrooms, chanterelle mushrooms, morels, porcini

Porcini

Porcini are in season in late summer, my favourite time of the year for creating new recipes because of the abundance of good produce. For most mushroom lovers, porcini are the ultimate prize. They have a heavy, bulbous stem and a tight-fitting cap varying in colour from light beige to dark brown. Italian families feast on these wild mushrooms in season, sautéed with garlic, stirred into risotto, mixed with pasta or just with Parmesan and olive oil.

Dried mushrooms

Dried porcini and morels are a good standby in your storecupboard. Although they are expensive, you need only a tiny amount because the flavour is very concentrated. Before use, soak dried mushrooms in hot water for a few minutes, then drain, straining the liquid through a muslin-lined sieve – or, if you're careful, a sheet of kitchen paper – to catch the sediment. Use this strained liquid as part of the cooking liquid in your recipe.

Olive oil

Always use cold-pressed olive oil; nothing else will give you an authentic flavour. Choose ordinary olive oil for frying and extra virgin olive oil for dressings and for drizzling over finished dishes. If you invest in a particularly good bottle of extra virgin oil, reserve it for sprinkling, with a little coarse sea salt, over its perfect partners – grilled fish, vegetables, meat, beef carpaccio, pasta with garlic, fresh tomatoes, grilled bread, warm white beans, roasted peppers and baked potatoes.

The character and strength of olive oil varies greatly depending on where it is from. Tuscany produces some of the best oils around. Strong-flavoured, with peppery overtones, they are excellent with starchy foods such as bread, beans and potatoes. Ligurian oil, on the other hand, is light and buttery tasting – especially good with grilled fish. Puglia is the most commercial oil-producing region and therefore makes the cheapest oil. I remember my father making olive oil for the family when I was growing up in Abruzzo and, after all these years, I have still not found an oil to match it. But Del Verde is one of the best imported oils from this region and they also make great pasta.

Clockwise from top: extra virgin olive oil, green olives, virgin olive oil, black olives

It is very easy to make your own flavoured olive oil. Suitable flavourings include herbs such as rosemary, basil, parsley or wild fennel; garlic (use whole unpeeled cloves that have been bashed so the skin splits); and halved fresh chillies. Put some extra virgin olive oil in a pan with your chosen flavouring and one or two strips of lemon rind and heat to just below boiling point – do not allow the oil to bubble. Remove from the heat and leave to cool completely, then bottle the oil (you can strain it or leave the flavourings in). Alternatively use the flavoured oil to marinate vegetables or goat's cheese in large Kilner jars.

Olives

The range of olives now available is quite daunting. All olives are green when unripe. As they ripen, they go through a number of colour changes, such as red, brown and purple. Basically the less ripe the olive the more herbal the flavour will be, while riper olives have a buttery, pruney overtone.

Experiment with the type of olives you would like to eat – most delis will allow you to taste before buying. Canned pitted olives in brine are really too bland for either eating or cooking. A good olive to start with is the deep-purple, slightly pointed Greek Kalamata, which is sold in vinegar or oil. The Italian San Remo from Liguria is small and brown or purple in colour, with a subtle flavour that makes it a lovely nibble with drinks. Large, brown-green, fleshy Sicilian olives are easy to slice and good used in cooking.

Pasta

It is worth keeping a good selection of pasta shapes in your storecupboard. When buying pasta, ensure that it is made from 100 per cent durum wheat or that the packet says *semola di grano*, which is only produced in Italy. If it contains egg, it will also say *all'uovo*.

As a general rule, use long, thin pasta for fairly thick sauces, hollow or twisted shapes for chunky sauces, wide flat noodles for rich sauces and delicate shapes for light sauces. Tagliatelle is good served with meats – did you know that in Italy bolognese sauce is served with tagliatelle, not spaghetti? Tagliolini and capellini are much thinner versions of

Clockwise from top left: linguine, tagliatelle, pappardelle, spaghetti, penne, fusilli

tagliatelle and are best served in broth soups or with light, oil-based sauces. Fettuccine, again thinner than tagliatelle, is good with butter and cream sauces. Spaghetti is perfect for olive oil- and tomato-based sauces, as the slippery sauce keeps the strands of pasta separate. Keep a look out for spaghettini, too – it is slightly thinner than spaghetti and makes an ideal partner for shellfish sauces. Linguine and trenette are good with spicy, oil-based sauces and fast sauces such as pesto. The tubes, bucatini, rigatoni and penne, are all perfect for catching chunks of meat in heavier sauces. Other good pastas to serve with meat include conchiglie, fusilli and orecchiette. Farfalle is one of the few short pastas best suited to creamy sauces. It is also pretty good in cheesy bakes. Pappardelle, wider but shorter than tagliatelle, is traditionally served only with game sauces, such as hare or rabbit. *Del verde* is my favourite dry pasta. Made in Italy, it is now available in England.

Fresh or dried?

I would recommend using good-quality Italian dried pasta, as it keeps well and cooks perfectly. The fresh pasta ribbons or shapes available in supermarkets are no better than dried. However, fresh pasta made on the premises in a good Italian deli is unbeatable, especially the stuffed ones such as ravioli, cannelloni and tortelloni.

Cooking pasta

Allow 75–120 g (3–4½ oz) pasta per person, whether it is fresh or dried. Bring a large pan of well-salted water to a rolling boil, add the pasta and stir it once. Return the water to a rolling boil and then start timing it, stirring occasionally. The timing will vary according to the type of pasta but in general you should start checking after about 8 minutes, unless you are using a very thin, quick-cooking pasta such as capelli d'angelo. Pasta should be cooked until it is al dente – i.e. tender but still with a gentle, nutty texture to the bite. To test if it is al dente, take a piece of pasta out of the water and cut or bite a piece off. If there are any white spots on the cut surface it needs a little more cooking; test again after a minute.

It is not necessary to add oil to the cooking water if you use a big pan with lots of bubbling water and stir the pasta several times. One of the main disadvantages of adding oil to the water is that it makes the pasta too slippery, so the sauce cannot adhere to it.

If the pasta is to be mixed into a sauce, it is always a good idea to reserve about 150 ml (¼ pint) of the cooking water in case you need to loosen the sauce a little once it has been mixed with the pasta.

When you are cooking pasta to use in salads, do not be tempted to cool it under cold running water, as this not only washes all the flavour out but saturates the pasta, giving it a thick macaroni look and taste. Instead you should drain the pasta and spread it out on a large tray or table top, then drizzle it with oil and stir gently to separate the pasta. Because of the large surface area, the pasta will cool very quickly.

Pesto

Pesto is often thought of as just a pasta sauce but it has many other great flavouring roles, too. Try teaming it with grilled vegetables, baked potatoes, blanched green beans (see Gnocchi with Pesto and Green Beans, page 60), grilled bread, fish or meat.

You should be able to find fresh pesto in good delis and some supermarkets. Although the classic version is made with basil, it is now fashionable to experiment with other flavours, such as coriander, parsley and red pesto (using red basil leaves). Wild rocket pesto is exceptionally good; just substitute wild rocket for basil in the recipe below.

Fresh pesto made at home is fast and extremely easy to prepare, especially if you have a food processor. Alternatively use a pestle and mortar, or even grind the ingredients in a bowl with the end of a rolling pin or a bottle. The quantities below will make about 300 ml (½ pint) pesto.

25 g (1 oz) fresh basil leaves
2 tablespoons pine nuts
2 garlic cloves, finely chopped
250 ml (8 fl oz) extra virgin olive oil
25 g (1 oz) Parmesan cheese, freshly grated
75 g (3 oz) pecorino cheese, freshly grated
salt and freshly ground black pepper

Grind the basil leaves with the pine nuts and garlic, adding a little of the olive oil. Gradually grind in the Parmesan and pecorino, drizzling in a little more oil between each addition. Season with salt and pepper.

If using a food processor, whiz all the ingredients except the oil to a paste, then, while the machine is still running, add the oil in a steady stream.

Pine nuts

These are little creamy-white seeds rather than nuts, taken from the cones of a Mediterranean pine tree. Their delicate flavour and aroma makes them suitable for desserts as well as savoury dishes. They are also used for making pesto. Pine nuts should be stored in the fridge, as they can turn rancid soon after opening.

Toasting pine nuts brings out their flavour. Just heat a dry frying pan over a moderate heat, add the nuts and cook for 3 or 4 minutes, shaking the pan several times, until golden brown.

Polenta flour

This is a type of cornmeal, or maize, which is usually cooked in plenty of water to make a thick porridge. It can be eaten immediately, while 'wet', or poured on to a board and left to set, then cut into slices and fried. Although polenta is an ancient food of Italy, it was originally made from a mush of different

From top: risotto rice, pine nuts

Clockwise from left: chicory, radicchio, rocket

grains, not corn. It was only when corn was brought back to Europe from the New World that the Italians re-taught themselves to make one of their favourite dishes.

Polenta flour is available in all large super-markets, delis and good food shops. Do not be tempted to use instant, or quick-cooking, polenta – it is just not the same.

Alternative uses of polenta flour include coating chicken or fish in it before frying or roasting – try coating a whole chicken in polenta before roasting, for a magical result – or substituting it for all or some of the flour in cakes.

Risotto rice

There are several varieties of risotto rice, all produced in Italy and classified as *superfino*. It contains amylopectin, a fast-dissolving starch that makes the rice sticky, and can absorb up to five times its weight in liquid without breaking up, making it uniquely suitable for classic Italian risotto. Good varieties to use are arborio, from Piedmont, and carnaroli, both of which are readily available in supermarkets and delicatessens.

Salad leaves
Chicory
Also known as Belgian endive, this has a small, compact head with smooth, crunchy leaves. It is commonly yellowish white but, depending on the season, you can find red chicory, too.

Radicchio
There are two types of radicchio. The most widely available is the small, tight, round shape known as Verona radicchio. It is a deep purplish-red and sometimes has white veins running through it. Alternatively there is the long, deep-red Treviso radicchio, which is shaped like a Cos lettuce but has much smoother leaves. Both have a slightly bitter flavour, as they come from the chicory family.

Radicchio is often used in salads but is also excellent grilled and dressed with extra virgin olive oil, balsamic vinegar and shavings of Parmesan cheese.

Rocket
Also known as arugula or roquette, this can be used as a salad leaf or a herb. The frillier the leaf, the more peppery it will taste. All supermarkets and many greengrocers stock rocket nowadays.

Saffron
This is the tiny stamen of the crocus flower. It has a unique aroma and gives food a beautiful yellow colour. In Italy it is most commonly used in risottos, fish stews and soups.
I recommend that you buy saffron strands rather than the powdered form, as the latter tends to be less pungent and is sometimes mixed with turmeric, which will enhance the colour but give a curry flavour.

Tomatoes
Fresh
Plum tomatoes are most commonly used in sauces in Italy since they are the juiciest variety, but they are not the tastiest. For salads, try to buy vine-ripened tomatoes, preferably organic, which can have a superb flavour. Simply dress them with good olive oil and sprinkle with sea salt flakes and freshly ripped basil. Look out for cherry tomatoes on the vine. They are packed with flavour and make delicious sauces.

To skin and seed tomatoes, make a small incision at the top of each, then put the tomatoes in a bowl and pour over plenty of boiling water from the kettle. Leave for 1–2 minutes, depending on how ripe the tomatoes are, then drain and cool under cold water. Pat dry and peel away the skin. Halve the tomatoes and scoop out the seeds, then dice the flesh.

Tinned

Tinned Italian plum tomatoes make a well-flavoured sauce but do remember to add a little soft brown sugar to balance their acidity.

Sun-dried

These are one of my favourite ingredients, as they add so much flavour. Until recently, the only sun-dried tomatoes available were the 'cardboard' variety that needed to be soaked before use. Now you can also get ones marinated in oil to use in salads or quick-cooking dishes, plus a newer variety – semi-dried tomatoes. Also known as sun-blushed tomatoes, these are quartered and marinated in oil and herbs. They are available in good food shops and some supermarkets and are excellent served on bruschetta, in salads or as easy drinks nibbles.

Wines

As there are over 2,000 grape varieties in Italy, there obviously isn't space here to cover all the wines available. Instead I have mentioned just a few from my own region of Abruzzo, as well as some of my other favourites.

A classic white wine from Abruzzo is the Trebbiano d'Abruzzo, also known as Abruzzo Bianco. It is a lovely, fresh, light wine, best served with seafood. Montepulciano is the main red wine grape grown in the Abruzzo region. With its deep, rich colour and dry, peppery-spicy finish, this medium-to full-bodied wine makes an excellent accompaniment to pasta and game dishes, as well as white meats. The best make has to be Illuminati. Chianti, produced in Tuscany, is possibly the best known of all Italian wines. There are many different styles, ranging from light Beaujolais-style quaffing wines, to structured, complex examples with enough backbone to justify ageing. The cheaper the Chianti, the rougher it will taste. I would recommend spending slightly more in order to get a mellower-flavoured wine.

Clockwise from top left: plum tomato, sun-dried tomato, baby plum tomato, vine-ripened tomato

Emilia-Romagna is the home of Parmesan cheese, balsamic vinegar and Lambrusco wine. Lambrusco wines are surprisingly underrated – I would certainly recommend the more expensive dry varieties (not the screw-tops!). When they are served chilled, they are ideal for barbecues and go well with chicken dishes.

When in Rome, or eating Roman dishes, I suggest you do as the Romans do and drink local wines. Rome is situated in the region of Lazio, which is one of Italy's most productive wine areas. Try its range of Frascatis, white wines that vary from dry to semi-dry to sweet, or the rather strangely named Est! Est! Est! from Montefiascone, which is a straw-yellow Muscat wine.

In most of Italy Marsala is thought of as a cooking wine but in its native Sicily it is regarded as a liqueur wine. It is often used in desserts, most notably zabaglione (see page 108). I would suggest investing in a good bottle of Marsala at Christmas, as it makes a perfect festive drink.

Venice is Italy's leading producer of classified wines (*denominazione di origine controllata*, or DOC, the equivalent of the French *appellation contrôlée*), with its Veneto trio of Soave, Bardolino and Valpolicella.

Soave, a dry white, should be drunk young, and not after its first year. It is made up of two different grape varieties and is the ideal wine for a hot summer's day if served really well chilled.

Bardolino is another blended wine, a dry, slightly bitter and sometimes slightly fizzy red. Valpolicella is well known internationally for its dry, velvety, full-bodied palate, with an aroma of spiced fruit. This is a fantastically smooth wine, which complements strong cheeses and is a great way to round off a meal.

Centerbe, whose name means 'a hundred herbs', is a powerful 70 per cent proof liqueur. It has a unique flavour and is considered a good remedy for colds and other illnesses. Aurum is another excellent liqueur, produced in the fishing town of Pescara, in the Abruzzo region.

EQUIPMENT

Italian cooking is very straightforward and you do not need loads of specialist equipment. However, there are a few items that will make life easier for you.

Cheese grater
Parmesan and pecorino cheese should be very finely grated, so opt for either a rotary grater or a box grater that includes a fine grating section.

Colander
A good-quality large metal colander with one or two sturdy handles is a must for pasta and vegetables. A sieve will be too small or too weak for draining heavy pasta and rice.

Food processor
This really does make life simpler. My mother used to be forever passing minestrones through sieves; one minute in the processor and the job is done. Food processors can also be used to make pesto, grind nuts, and mix cakes and pasta dough.

Griddle pan
Also called a chargrill pan, this is made of cast iron and has a ridged surface that holds the food above any fat in the pan and gives it attractive dark-brown marks. Food cooked on a hot griddle pan develops a slightly smoky flavour, as if it had been cooked on a barbecue. It is an ideal way of searing meat, firm-textured fish, and vegetables. If your griddle has an ovenproof handle you can transfer it to the oven to finish off the cooking. Before use, always heat the griddle until it is starting to smoke and oil the food lightly before putting it in the pan.

Ovenproof frying pan
A wide frying pan, at least 7.5 cm (3 in) deep, with an ovenproof handle can be transferred from hob to oven, enabling you to brown and seal food such as steak or fish, then finish them off in the oven for more even cooking. It is also perfect for pasta sauces, since it has a large surface area to allow the cooking juices to evaporate quickly and plenty of room to add the pasta to the sauce.

Food processor, griddle pan, pasta spoon, colander

Pestle and mortar, scales, cheese grater, spatula

Pasta pan, ovenproof frying pan, tongs

Pasta pan

For cooking pasta you need a large, light, deep pan that will allow you to boil lots of water quickly and is not too heavy to lift when full.

Pestle and mortar

For perfect pesto, a mortar (bowl section) and pestle (hand masher) are essential. They can be made of marble, clay or wood. You can also crush garlic in a mortar with a little sea salt to help break it down. I like using a pestle and mortar for roughly crushing small amounts of nuts and peppercorns.

Scales

Do invest in a good set of scales. The digital ones are the most flexible and easiest to read, whether you use Imperial or metric measurements. Weighing ingredients accurately is very important when making desserts, especially cakes, and polenta.

Spatula

Long-handled plastic spatulas are useful for easy access to ingredients in a food processor and for scraping pudding and cake mixtures out of bowls.

Tongs

Tongs allow you to pick up meats of all shapes and sizes with a good grip and turn them over in one go. They also allow you to pick up a strand of pasta or just one pasta tube to test if it is al dente, and are invaluable for tossing and serving pasta. Choose ones with a long handle so you don't risk burning your hands.

Conversion tables

Conversions are approximate and have been rounded up or down. Follow one set of measurements only – do not mix metric and Imperial.

Weights		Volume		Measurements	
Metric	**Imperial**	**Metric**	**Imperial**	**Metric**	**Imperial**
15 g	½ oz	25 ml	1 fl oz	0.5 cm	¼ inch
25 g	1 oz	50 ml	2 fl oz	1 cm	½ inch
40 g	1½ oz	85 ml	3 fl oz	2.5 cm	1 inch
50 g	2 oz	150 ml	5 fl oz (¼ pint)	5 cm	2 inches
75 g	3 oz	300 ml	10 fl oz (½ pint)	7.5 cm	3 inches
100 g	4 oz	450 ml	15 fl oz (¾ pint)	10 cm	4 inches
150 g	5 oz	600 ml	1 pint	15 cm	6 inches
175 g	6 oz	700 ml	1¼ pints	18 cm	7 inches
200 g	7 oz	900 ml	1½ pints	20 cm	8 inches
225 g	8 oz	1 litres	1¾ pints	23 cm	9 inches
250 g	9 oz	1.2 litres	2 pints	25 cm	10 inches
275 g	10 oz	1.25 litres	2¼ pints	30 cm	12 inches
350 g	12 oz	1.5 litres	2½ pints		
375 g	13 oz	1.6 litres	2¾ pints	**Oven temperatures**		
400 g	14 oz	1.75 litres	3 pints	140°C	275°F	Gas Mk 1
425 g	15 oz	1.8 litres	3¼ pints	150°C	300°F	Gas Mk 2
450 g	1 lb	2 litres	3½ pints	160°C	325°F	Gas Mk 3
550 g	1¼ lb	2.1 litres	3¾ pints	180°C	350°F	Gas Mk 4
675 g	1½ lb	2.25 litres	4 pints	190°C	375°F	Gas Mk 5
900 g	2 lb	2.75 litres	5 pints	200°C	400°F	Gas Mk 6
1.5 kg	3 lb	3.4 litres	6 pints	220°C	425°F	Gas Mk 7
1.75 kg	4 lb	3.9 litres	7 pints	230°C	450°F	Gas Mk 8
2.25 kg	5 lb	5 litres	8 pints (1 gal)	240°C	475°F	Gas Mk 9

SOUPS and STARTERS

Tuscan bean soup with pasta

This is a great winter warmer served with some crusty ciabatta bread. On a business trip to Florence I discovered a restaurant called Latini. It doesn't have a menu and it serves this soup as a starter before its famous Florentine steak with a flask of red wine – what a feast! From May onwards you can find fresh borlotti beans in good greengrocers' and some Italian delis that also stock fresh produce. The fresh beans really do taste good but canned beans are an easy substitute.

serves 4
preparation time: 25 minutes
cooking time: 1 hour 10 minutes

4 tablespoons extra virgin olive oil

350 g (12 oz) piece of ham or knuckle bone, thick skin trimmed

2 red onions, sliced into fine rings

1–2 garlic cloves, crushed

6 plum tomatoes, skinned, seeded and chopped

1 red chilli, finely chopped (optional)

1.2 litres (2 pints) water

675 g (1½ lb) fresh borlotti beans, shelled, or 2 x 400 g (14 oz) cans of borlotti beans, drained and rinsed

200 g (7 oz) ditalini pasta or maccheroni

4 fresh basil leaves, torn

salt and freshly ground black pepper

freshly grated Parmesan cheese and crusty Italian bread, to serve

1 Heat 2 tablespoons of the olive oil in a large pan and brown the ham or knuckle bone for 5 minutes, turning regularly. Stir in the onions, garlic, tomatoes and chilli, if using, and sauté for 3 minutes.

2 Pour in the water and bring to the boil, skimming off any scum from the surface. Simmer for 45 minutes. Always have a bowl of cold water so you can clean your solid spoon as you skim.

5 Stir in the remaining olive oil and season to taste. Serve in deep bowls, with grated Parmesan cheese for sprinkling and some crusty Italian bread.

3 Remove the ham or knuckle bone from the pan and scrape the meat, trimming the fat off. Chop the meat and place it in a food processor with the soup. Blend until smooth (you may need to do this in 2 batches).

4 Return the soup to the pan and bring back to the boil. Stir in the beans, bring to a simmer and cook for 10 minutes. Then add the pasta and torn basil leaves and cook for 5–6 minutes or until the pasta is tender.

Minestrone of rice and vegetables

The pancetta can be left out to make this vegetarian. Please yourself as to which vegetables you use but I would stick to ones in season. Aubergines and peppers are best avoided as they might be overpowering. Good greengrocers stock wild broccoli from April (use the long stems and florets) and tender, fresh broad beans arrive in late March until June or July.

serves 6
preparation time: 20 minutes
cooking time: 30 minutes

4 tablespoons extra virgin olive oil

50 g (2 oz) pancetta, diced

1 large onion, diced

2 garlic cloves, crushed

2 medium carrots, diced

2 celery sticks, diced

2 courgettes, diced

100 g (4 oz) broccoli (preferably wild), trimmed into florets, stems peeled and chopped

4 plum tomatoes, skinned, seeded and diced

1.2 litres (2 pints) vegetable stock

450 g (1 lb) fresh broad beans, podded, or 300 g (11 oz) frozen broad beans

150 g (5 oz) rice

40 g (1½ oz) pecorino romano cheese, grated

salt and freshly ground black pepper

crusty Italian bread, to serve

1 Heat 2 tablespoons of the olive oil in a large, heavy-based pan, stir in the pancetta and onion and cook gently for 5 minutes, until the onion is soft.

2 Add the garlic, carrots, celery, courgettes, broccoli stalks (but not the florets) and tomatoes. Fry for 5–7 minutes, stirring frequently, until the vegetables look bright in colour.

3 Pour in the stock and bring to the boil. Stir in the broad beans and rice and season with salt and pepper. Simmer for 10 minutes, or until the rice is just tender.

4 Add the broccoli florets and cook for 5 minutes. Stir in the remaining olive oil and the pecorino cheese. Serve immediately, with crusty Italian bread.

Tiger prawns on skewers

Most fishmongers and big supermarkets stock Mediterranean, Madagascan or Thai tiger prawns. They vary in size, so if you are using very large ones allow three per person; if they are slightly smaller you will need five per serving. You will also need four wooden skewers that have been soaked in water for about 30 minutes before use to prevent them burning.

serves 4
preparation time: 20 minutes,
    plus 10 minutes' marinating
cooking time: 10 minutes

12 large raw tiger prawns, or
    20 smaller ones

75 g (3 oz) bag of small
    mixed salad leaves

2 ripe plum tomatoes,
    skinned, seeded and diced

1 tablespoon chopped fresh
    flat-leaf parsley

freshly ground black pepper

1 lemon, cut into wedges, to
    serve

For the marinade:

3 tablespoons extra virgin
    olive oil

1 teaspoon salt

juice of 1 lemon

1 teaspoon finely grated fresh
    root ginger

1 garlic clove, finely chopped

1 red chilli, seeded and finely
    chopped

For the dressing:

3 tablespoons extra virgin
    olive oil

juice of 1 lemon

1 red chilli, seeded and sliced

2 sprigs of fresh rosemary

1 Remove the heads from the prawns and discard. Peel off the shell, leaving the small tail shell at the end still attached. Remove the black vein that lies along the outer curve of the prawn by carefully running a small, sharp knife around the curve and lifting out the vein with the tip of the knife.

2 Place the prawns in a bowl with all the marinade ingredients and mix well. Leave to marinate for 10 minutes.

3 Remove the prawns from the marinade and thread them on to the soaked wooden skewers. Place under a hot grill and cook for 4 minutes on each side, basting with the marinade occasionally.

4 Meanwhile, put all the ingredients for the dressing in a small pan and heat gently for 2 minutes.

5 Arrange the salad leaves on 4 serving plates and place a skewer of prawns on top. Discard the rosemary sprigs and spoon the warm dressing over the prawns. Scatter the tomatoes on top, then the chopped parsley and some freshly ground black pepper. Serve with the lemon wedges.

Fennel, radicchio and gorgonzola salad

Fennel has a great affinity with citrus fruits. Here, a tangy lemon dressing with sweet, aniseedy fennel and a few bitter leaves makes a winning combination. Fennel teamed with orange also works well.This very simple but quite filling salad is very good served by itself as a starter or makes an excellent accompaniment to grilled or barbecued fish in summer.

serves 4
preparation time: 15 minutes

2 fennel bulbs

2 heads of radicchio

1 head of chicory

25 g (1 oz) walnuts, chopped

50 g (2 oz) gorgonzola cheese, chopped

4 tablespoons extra virgin olive oil

2 tablespoons fresh lemon juice

1 garlic clove, finely chopped

1 tablespoon chopped fresh parsley

salt and freshly ground black pepper

lemon wedges, to serve

1 Cut the feathery fronds from the fennel and reserve, then trim away the hard outer layer of the fennel bulbs.

2 Roughly shred the radicchio, chicory and fennel. Place them in a large, shallow bowl and sprinkle over the chopped walnuts and gorgonzola cheese.

3 To make the dressing, mix the olive oil with the lemon juice, garlic and parsley. Season with plenty of salt and pepper.

4 Pour the dressing over the salad and toss the leaves with your hands to mix them gently with the dressing. Garnish with the reserved fennel fronds and serve with lemon wedges.

Roasted vegetables with goat's cheese and basil oil

All Mediterranean vegetables taste sweet and mellow when roasted with olive oil and a little seasoning. Try pumpkin or butternut squash with pine nuts – remember these will need a little extra time to cook. If you prefer, you can omit the cheese from this simple recipe. Add a little balsamic vinegar instead and it will be just as good.

serves 4
preparation time: 25 minutes
cooking time: 25 minutes

1 aubergine
1 large or 2 small courgettes
1 fennel bulb
1 red pepper
1 yellow pepper
5 baby shallots
6 tablespoons olive oil
4 garlic cloves, peeled
4 slices of round, firm goat's cheese
sea salt flakes and freshly ground black pepper

For the basil oil:
6 tablespoons extra virgin olive oil
15 g (½ oz) fresh basil leaves, torn
juice of ½ lemon

1 Pre-heat the oven to 200°C/400°F/Gas Mark 6. Trim the aubergine, courgette and fennel and cut them into fairly large wedges. Cut the peppers into quarters and remove the seeds. Peel and halve the shallots.

2 Place all the vegetables in a roasting tin with the olive oil, garlic cloves and salt and pepper. Toss the vegetables with your hands, rubbing the oil and seasoning into them. Roast for 15–20 minutes, until softened but still slightly crunchy, stirring half way through.

4 Meanwhile, make the basil oil: put the oil, basil and lemon juice in a food processor or liquidizer and blend until smooth; the mixture will be lightly flecked with the basil. Transfer the roasted vegetables and goat's cheese to warmed serving plates, drizzle with the basil oil and serve.

3 Mix the vegetables once more, then top with the goat's cheese slices. Roast for another 5 minutes, until the cheese has just melted.

Mozzarella, rocket and roasted red peppers

A very simple, colourful salad that captures the essence of Italy. Buffalo mozzarella has a richer flavour and more melting texture than conventional cow's milk mozzarellas and is best eaten simply. The peppers can be prepared a few days in advance and stored in the fridge or, if you are short of time, you could buy ready-roasted peppers from a deli. There's no harm making life easier if you're not compromising on flavour!

serves 4
preparation time: 20 minutes
cooking time: 20 minutes

3 red peppers

2 sprigs of fresh rosemary

5 tablespoons extra virgin olive oil

1 tablespoon capers, rinsed and drained

75 g (3 oz) rocket

4 x 125 g (4½ oz) or 2 x 200 g (7 oz) buffalo mozzarella cheese, drained

salt and freshly ground black pepper

For the dressing:

1 teaspoon Dijon mustard

1 teaspoon mayonnaise

1 teaspoon honey

2 tablespoons fresh lemon juice

2 tablespoons extra virgin olive oil

1 Pre-heat the oven to 190°C/375°F/Gas Mark 5. Place the peppers in a roasting tin with a sprig of rosemary and drizzle over 1 tablespoon of the oil. Roast for 20 minutes, until the peppers are soft to the touch and just charred. Place them in a bowl, stretch clingfilm over them and leave to cool. Pour any juices from the roasting tin into a bowl and set aside.

2 When the peppers are cool, cut off the tops, pouring any juice from inside the peppers into the bowl of reserved juices. Remove the seeds and membranes, then peel off the skin. Slice the peppers and place in the bowl with the cooking juices.

3 Strip the leaves from the remaining rosemary sprig and chop them finely, then add to the roasted peppers with the capers and the remaining oil. Mix well and season to taste.

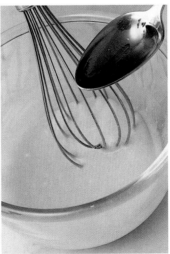

4 For the dressing, mix the mustard, mayonnaise and honey together, then add the lemon juice, whisking constantly to prevent it separating. Add the oil, whisking until the dressing has thickened slightly. Season to taste. Toss the rocket with the dressing. If using 4 small mozzarellas, halve them and place 2 halves on each plate. Put the peppers next to the mozzarella and rocket, and spoon over the extra juices.

Polenta with wild and field mushrooms

Polenta has been part of Italian cooking for many years and has recently made a great comeback because it is so versatile. My mother's favourite way of serving it was with grilled sausages and this wonderful mushroom sauce.

serves 8
preparation time: 25 minutes
cooking time: 40 minutes

Like most polenta dishes, this is quite filling. Serve a wedge per person as a starter or serve as a main course for four people. If you like, the polenta can be served 'wet' – i.e. before it sets – instead of being griddled.

Cooked set polenta freezes well. Thaw when required and gently heat it in the oven before griddling. If you griddle the polenta when it is cold, it will stick to the pan and will not heat through evenly. Ready-cooked polenta that only needs to be sliced is available in supermarkets. It makes life easier but the flavour of home-made polenta is far superior.

5 tablespoons extra virgin olive oil

1 small onion, finely chopped

1 garlic clove, crushed

4 field mushrooms, brushed clean and sliced

175 g (6 oz) wild mushrooms, brushed clean (and sliced – unless they are already bite-sized)

4 tablespoons chopped fresh flat-leaf parsley

120 ml (4 fl oz) dry white wine such as Verdicchio

8 fresh basil leaves, chopped, plus a few torn basil leaves to garnish

salt and freshly ground black pepper

For the polenta:

1 litre (1¾ pints) water

2 teaspoons salt

175 g (6 oz) polenta flour

50 g (2 oz) butter

100 g (4 oz) Parmesan cheese, freshly grated

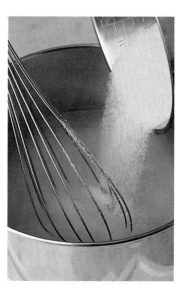

1 To make the polenta, put the water in a large, deep pan with the salt. Bring to the boil, then reduce the heat and gradually add the polenta, stirring constantly with a whisk.

2 Simmer for 20 minutes, stirring frequently, until the polenta is very thick and is coming away from the side of the pan; it may seem that the polenta has thickened faster than this but it really must cook on to allow the grains to become tender.

3 Beat the butter and Parmesan into the polenta and season to taste, adding plenty of black pepper. Pour the wet polenta into a 23–25 cm (9–10 in) round shallow tin and spread it evenly with a palette knife into a layer about 1 cm (½ in) thick. Leave to cool until set.

4 Heat 3 tablespoons of the olive oil in a large frying pan, add the onion and garlic and fry for 5 minutes, until soft and just starting to brown. Stir in the mushrooms and parsley and fry for 5–8 minutes, until the mushrooms are golden brown.

7 Brush the uncooked side with more oil, then gently turn the polenta over with a palette knife or fish slice. Cook for another 2–3 minutes, until toasted. Put a polenta wedge on each serving plate, spoon the mushroom mixture on top and sprinkle with some torn basil leaves. Serve immediately.

5 Add some salt and pepper, then the wine, and simmer for 5 minutes. Remove from the heat and stir in the chopped basil. Add more seasoning if necessary.

6 Cut the polenta into 8 wedges and brush the top with some of the remaining olive oil. Heat a ridged chargrill pan until very hot and place the polenta wedges on it, oiled-side down, pressing them on to the hot surface. Cook for 2–3 minutes, until golden.

PASTA
and RICE

Spaghetti with cherry tomato sauce

Sweet cherry tomatoes are a big hit with children – even more reason to use them! Depending on the season, golden cherry tomatoes might be available as well as red. Baby plum tomatoes are another well-flavoured variety. This sauce can also be made using ripe fresh plum tomatoes – although it will take a little longer, as you will have to skin and seed the tomatoes first. Add a teaspoon of sugar to balance the tomatoes' acidity.

serves 4
preparation time: 10 minutes
cooking time: 35 minutes

4 tablespoons olive oil

1 small onion, finely chopped

1 garlic clove, crushed

450 g (1 lb) cherry tomatoes

15 g (½ oz) fresh basil, torn into small pieces

about 1 teaspoon soft brown sugar (optional)

400 g (14 oz) spaghetti

½ vegetable stock cube

65 g (2½ oz) Parmesan cheese, freshly grated

salt and freshly ground black pepper

1 Heat the oil in a large, deep frying pan, add the onion and cook over a very low heat for about 5 minutes, until soft but not brown. Stir in the garlic, tomatoes and basil.

2 Cook over a low heat for 10 minutes, until the tomatoes have softened, then mash them gently with the back of a wooden spoon. Continue to simmer for 20 minutes, until the sauce is very thick. Season with salt and pepper to taste, adding the sugar if needed to balance the acidity of the tomatoes.

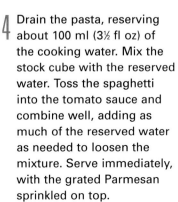

3 Meanwhile, bring a large pan of salted water to a rolling boil. Add the spaghetti, gently easing it into the water. Return to a gentle rolling boil and cook for 10–12 minutes, until al dente, stirring occasionally.

4 Drain the pasta, reserving about 100 ml (3½ fl oz) of the cooking water. Mix the stock cube with the reserved water. Toss the spaghetti into the tomato sauce and combine well, adding as much of the reserved water as needed to loosen the mixture. Serve immediately, with the grated Parmesan sprinkled on top.

Linguine with saffron, prawns and salmon

This is one of our best sellers at Zilli Fish. The delicate saffron flavour combined with sweet-tasting prawns and salmon is perfect in this creamy, but light sauce. The secret is not to overcook the cream, or it will curdle. It is a good idea to reserve a little of the pasta cooking water before draining; use this to loosen the sauce if necessary once the pasta has been added. Make sure that you undercook the salmon initially as it will continue to cook once added to the sauce.

serves 4
preparation time: 20 minutes
cooking time: 20 minutes

350 g (12 oz) thick salmon fillet

200 ml (7 fl oz) dry white wine such as Trebbiano

1 tablespoon extra virgin olive oil

1 tablespoon chopped fresh basil, plus a few torn basil leaves to garnish

6 ripe Italian plum tomatoes, skinned, seeded and finely diced

150 ml (¼ pint) double cream

a pinch of saffron strands

350 g (12 oz) linguine

100 g (4 oz) small peeled cooked prawns

sea salt flakes and freshly ground black pepper

1 Pre-heat the grill to high or pre-heat the oven to 200°C/400°F/Gas Mark 6. Place the salmon skin-side down in a baking tin and drizzle with a splash of the wine and the oil. Sprinkle with the chopped basil and season with salt and pepper. Grill or roast for 8 minutes, until just beginning to brown on top but still quite underdone in the centre. Set aside to cool.

2 Bring a large pan of salted water to the boil for the pasta. Meanwhile, put the tomatoes and cream in a large pan and bring to the boil, stirring well. Lower the heat and simmer for 2 minutes, then add the saffron and the remaining wine. Simmer for 5–7 minutes, until reduced and slightly thickened.

3 Add the pasta to the boiling salted water, easing it in gently. Stir and return to a gentle rolling boil, then cook for 8–10 minutes, until al dente. Meanwhile, flake the salmon into fairly large chunks, discarding the skin.

4 Add the salmon and prawns to the sauce and stir until the fish is well coated. Season to taste. Drain the pasta, reserving a little of the cooking liquid, and add to the sauce. Toss to combine. If the sauce is too thick, add some of the reserved pasta water. Serve immediately, garnishing with some torn basil leaves.

Rigatoni with traditional pork bolognese

Old favourites like this are always popular with the boys in Zilli Bar. I prefer to use pork but beef is more usual. The key to this sauce is time: make sure you leave it on a low heat for about an hour. In Italy, the amount of sauce should be equal to or less than the pasta, while in the UK it is usual to have a lot more sauce. If this is how you prefer it, increase the pork quantity to 450 g (1 lb) and add 150 ml (¼ pint) meat stock.

serves 4
preparation time: 15 minutes
cooking time: 1 hour 20 minutes

2 tablespoons olive oil

40 g (1½ oz) butter

1 onion, finely chopped

1 celery stick, finely chopped

1 carrot, finely diced

250 g (9 oz) lean minced pork

200 ml (7 fl oz) full-bodied red wine such as Montepulciano d'Abruzzo

400 g (14 oz) can of chopped tomatoes

2 tablespoons chopped fresh flat-leaf parsley

a little flour, mixed to a paste with water (optional)

350 g (12 oz) rigatoni

salt and freshly ground black pepper

freshly grated Parmesan cheese, to serve

1 Heat the oil and butter in a deep pan, add the onion, celery and carrot and stir well. Cook over a gentle heat for 5 minutes, until just beginning to soften.

2 Increase the heat and add the minced pork. Cook for 10 minutes, stirring constantly for the first 3 minutes to break up the lumps. Add the red wine and simmer for 3 minutes.

3 Stir in the tomatoes and season well with salt and pepper. Partially cover and cook over a low heat for 1 hour, stirring occasionally, until the meat and vegetables are very tender and the juices have thickened. Stir in the parsley. (If the sauce isn't thick enough, add a little flour and water paste and cook for a further 5–10 minutes.)

4 Bring a large pan of salted water to a rolling boil. Add the rigatoni, stir and return to a gently rolling boil. Cook for 10–12 minutes, until al dente, then drain. Add the pasta to the sauce and mix well. Serve in deep bowls with a sprinkling of Parmesan.

Angel hair pasta, vegetables and smoked mozzarella

Angel hair pasta, or *capelli d'angelo*, cooks so fast that you have to make sure everything else is ready before cooking it. Once the pasta is in the pan, stir it regularly to separate the nests and prevent them sticking together. Make sure the vegetables are sliced or diced finely, so they cook quickly and complement the delicate pasta.

serves 4
preparation time: 15 minutes
cooking time: 20 minutes

1 tablespoon extra virgin olive oil

50 g (2 oz) butter

1 onion, finely chopped

1 large carrot, peeled

1 celery stick, trimmed

1 red pepper, seeded, white membranes removed

2 yellow peppers, seeded, white membranes removed

150 g (5 oz) mascarpone cheese

350 g (12 oz) angel hair pasta

½ vegetable stock cube

200 g (7 oz) smoked mozzarella, peeled and diced

sea salt flakes and freshly ground black pepper

extra virgin olive oil and balsamic vinegar, to serve

1 Heat the oil and butter in a large, deep frying pan, add the onion and cook for 5 minutes, until golden. Meanwhile, finely dice or slice the carrot, celery and peppers.

2 Add the vegetables to the pan and cook gently for 8–10 minutes, stirring frequently, until tender. Season well with salt and pepper, then stir in the mascarpone cheese until it has melted.

3 Meanwhile, bring a large pan of salted water to the boil. Once the vegetables are ready, add the pasta to the boiling water and stir well with a large fork to separate the strands. Cook for 3 minutes, until al dente, then drain, reserving 150 ml (¼ pint) of the cooking water.

4 Stir the vegetable stock cube into the reserved cooking water until dissolved. Add the pasta to the vegetables and toss well, using some of the reserved water to loosen the mixture.

5 Stir in the diced mozzarella, allowing it to melt. Adjust the seasoning if necessary. Divide the pasta between 4 serving bowls and drizzle with some extra virgin olive oil and balsamic vinegar to serve.

Tagliatelle carbonara

Many chefs have their own version of this famous dish. You will find that you'll never buy a ready-made sauce again if you make this recipe yourself, so give it a go. You shouldn't need to add any extra salt as bacon and Parmesan are naturally salty and will season the dish for you.

serves 4

preparation time: 15 minutes

cooking time: 10 minutes

75 g (3 oz) butter

100 g (4 oz) pancetta or unsmoked bacon, cut into strips

400 g (14 oz) tagliatelle

8 egg yolks

6 tablespoons double cream

50 g (2 oz) Parmesan cheese, freshly grated

1 small teaspoon freshly ground black pepper

½ teaspoon freshly grated nutmeg

2 tablespoons chopped fresh parsley

1 Bring a large pan of salted water to the boil for the pasta. Melt the butter in a large, deep frying pan, add the pancetta and cook over a medium heat for a few minutes, until golden brown.

2 Add the pasta to the boiling salted water, stir and return to a gentle rolling boil. Cook for 8 minutes until al dente. Meanwhile, in a bowl large enough to hold the pasta, mix together the egg yolks, cream, Parmesan, pepper, nutmeg and parsley.

3 Drain the pasta. Remove the pancetta from the heat and add the pasta to it, mixing quickly with the bacon and butter.

4 Add the pasta mixture to the egg mixture and toss well. The heat from the bacon, butter and pasta will cook the egg yolks. You must serve the dish immediately or the eggs will curdle.

Gnocchi with pesto and green beans

Gnocchi are Italian potato dumplings, served like pasta. You should always try and make your own gnocchi, as the taste is so much better than the vacuum-packed ones you can buy.

serves 4 as a main course,
8 as a starter
preparation time: 50 minutes
cooking time: 45 minutes

The secret of making gnocchi at home is to use starchy, floury potatoes such as King Edwards and boil them in their skins to prevent excess water entering the potato flesh. If liked, the potatoes can be placed in a warm oven for 5 minutes after draining to dry out a bit more – the drier the mash, the better the gnocchi.

Uncooked gnocchi freeze very well and can be cooked straight from the freezer. Pesto sauce makes the perfect partner for gnocchi; other sauces that would go well include cherry tomato sauce (see page 48) and the saffron, prawn and salmon served with linguine on page 50.

1 kg (2¼ lb) large floury potatoes, such as King Edwards

2 egg yolks

200 g (7 oz) plain flour

1 litre (1¾ pints) water or chicken stock, for poaching

500 g (1 lb 2 oz) young green beans

1 quantity of home-made Pesto (see page 15), or use good-quality bought fresh pesto

salt

extra virgin olive oil and torn fresh basil leaves, to garnish

freshly grated Parmesan cheese, to serve

1 Cook the unpeeled potatoes in a large pan of boiling salted water for 30 minutes or until tender. Drain and leave until just cool enough to handle, then peel. Mash the potatoes or press them through a potato ricer or sieve into a bowl.

4 Place each piece on a fork and, gently pressing down with your thumb, roll it off the fork on to the board. The tines of the fork should leave grooves on one side of the gnocchi.

2 Season the mashed potato with salt and beat in the egg yolks, then beat in the flour a little at a time. This will form a smooth, slightly sticky dough.

3 Tip the dough out on to a well-floured board, then, with your hands, roll it into long sausage shapes about 1 cm (½ in) thick. Cut into sections about 2 cm (¾ in) long.

5 Bring the water or stock to the boil in a large pan and add a batch of gnocchi. Simmer until they rise to the surface, then cook for another 50–60 seconds. Using a slotted spoon, transfer them to a large bowl. Keep warm while you cook the remaining gnocchi.

6 Cook the green beans in a pan of boiling salted water until just tender, then drain well.

7 Mix the pesto and green beans together and spoon them into serving bowls. Top with the gnocchi, drizzle with a little extra virgin olive oil and sprinkle with torn basil leaves. Serve with a dish of grated Parmesan or with the gnocchi and sauce mixed together. Either way it is delicious.

Sun-dried tomato, goat's cheese and rocket risotto

This risotto has a clean, white finish from the melting goat's cheese, speckled with the red sun-dried tomatoes and bright green rocket. If possible, it tastes even better than it looks! Soft, fresh goat's cheeses are not suitable for this dish. A good cheese to use is one that comes in small thick rounds with an edible rind – this can be easily sliced for grilling without losing its shape.

serves 4
preparation time: 15 minutes
cooking time: 30 minutes

1 litre (1¾ pints) chicken or vegetable stock

100 g (4 oz) butter

1 large onion, chopped

1 bay leaf

350 g (12 oz) arborio or carnaroli risotto rice

200 ml (7 fl oz) dry white wine such as Verdicchio

100 g (4 oz) goat's cheese, diced, plus 4 slices of goat's cheese for grilling

100 g (4 oz) sun-dried tomatoes in oil, drained and sliced

50 g (2 oz) rocket, chopped

25 g (1 oz) Parmesan cheese, freshly grated

salt and freshly ground black pepper

1 Heat the stock in a saucepan and keep it at a simmer. Melt 75 g (3 oz) of the butter in a large, deep frying pan, add the onion and bay leaf and cook gently for 5 minutes, until the onion is soft. Add the rice and stir until all the grains are glistening with butter.

2 Add the white wine and simmer for 2 minutes, until it has evaporated. Add a ladleful of hot stock and cook over a moderate heat, stirring, until it has been absorbed. Continue adding the stock in this way until it has all, or nearly all, been used up and the rice is al dente, which should take about 18–20 minutes.

3 About 5 minutes before the risotto is cooked, stir in the diced goat's cheese, sun-dried tomatoes and rocket. Cook for 3–5 minutes, adding more stock as needed. The cheese should not melt completely.

4 Add the remaining butter and the Parmesan to the risotto and season to taste. The finished risotto should be quite fluffy and loose enough to form a wave, but not soupy. Remove from the heat, cover and leave for 1 minute.

5 Meanwhile, put the slices of goat's cheese on a foil-lined grill pan and place under a preheated grill for 1–2 minutes, until golden. Serve each portion of risotto with a slice of grilled goat's cheese on top, finished with a twist of black pepper.

Radicchio and fennel risotto

Radicchio and fennel make a fantastic salad (see page 32) and a pretty good risotto, too. The radicchio wilts and turns a deep rustic colour, giving the risotto a mellow, autumnal look. The delicate balance of bitter leaves, aromatic fennel and zingy lemon zest is marvellous. Make sure you use a good Parmesan cheese so as not to overpower these flavours.

serves 4
preparation time: 25 minutes
cooking time: 30 minutes

1 litre (1¾ pints) vegetable stock

90 g (3½oz) butter

225 g (8 oz) fennel, finely sliced

6 shallots, finely chopped

350 g (12 oz) arborio or carnaroli risotto rice

120 ml (4 fl oz) medium red wine

175 g (6 oz) radicchio, shredded

finely grated zest of 2 lemons

15 g (½ oz) fresh flat-leaf parsley, finely chopped

15 g (½ oz) fresh basil leaves, torn

75 g (3 oz) Parmesan cheese, freshly grated, plus extra to serve if liked

sea salt and freshly ground black pepper

1 Bring the stock to a simmer in a saucepan and keep hot. Melt half the butter in a large, deep frying pan, add the fennel and shallots and cook gently for 5 minutes, until tender.

2 Add the rice and stir well until it is glistening with butter. Add the wine and shredded radicchio and season with pepper. Cook for 2 minutes, until the wine has evaporated.

3 Add a ladleful of hot stock to the rice and cook over a moderate heat, stirring, until it has been absorbed. Continue adding the stock in this fashion, stirring constantly, until it has all, or nearly all, been used and the rice is just tender. This should take about 18–20 minutes.

4 Remove the risotto from the heat and stir in the lemon zest, parsley, basil, Parmesan and the remaining butter. The finished risotto should be quite fluffy and loose enough to form a wave, but not soupy. Cover and leave to rest for 1 minute, then stir again. Serve with more Parmesan if required.

Pumpkin and jumbo prawn risotto

The possible flavourings for risotto are as endless as sauces for pasta. Pumpkin is a big favourite of mine and very popular with children, as is butternut squash. I prefer to use jumbo tiger prawns in this recipe as they give a much fuller flavour than smaller prawns. Cold leftover risotto can be shaped into small balls, coated in flour, beaten egg and dried breadcrumbs, and deep-fried or baked. Serve with a salad or as party nibbles.

serves 4
preparation time: 20 minutes
cooking time: 40 minutes

2 tablespoons extra virgin olive oil

50 g (2 oz) butter

6 shallots, finely chopped

450 g (1 lb) pumpkin or butternut squash, peeled, seeded and cut into 1 cm (½ in) cubes

2 garlic cloves, crushed

1 litre (1¾ pints) fish or vegetable stock

350 g (12 oz) arborio or carnaroli risotto rice

120 ml (4 fl oz) dry white wine such as Trebbiano

4 large raw tiger prawns, peeled, de-veined (see page 28) and sliced

3 tablespoons chopped fresh flat-leaf parsley

4 tablespoons freshly grated Parmesan cheese

salt and freshly ground black pepper

1 Heat the oil and half the butter in a large, deep frying pan, add the shallots and fry gently for 5 minutes, until soft. Stir in the pumpkin or squash with the garlic and cook for about 8 minutes, until it starts to soften. Bring the stock to a simmer in a separate pan. Meanwhile, stir the rice into the pumpkin, making sure each grain is glistening with butter. Add the wine and cook for 2 minutes, until it has evaporated.

2 Add a ladleful of hot stock to the rice and cook over a moderate heat, stirring, for 3–5 minutes until it has been absorbed. Add the sliced prawns, stirring well, and season with salt and freshly ground black pepper.

4 When the risotto is done, remove from the heat and stir in the remaining butter, plus the parsley and Parmesan cheese. The finished risotto should be quite fluffy and loose enough to form a wave, but not soupy. Cover and leave to rest for 1 minute, then serve, with extra freshly ground black pepper.

3 Continue adding the stock a ladleful at a time, stirring constantly, until all or nearly all the stock has been used and the rice and pumpkin are tender. This should take about 18–20 minutes from adding the first ladleful of stock.

FISH and MEAT

Sea bass with a sea salt and black pepper crust

Sea bass is a delicately flavoured white fish with fairly firm flesh but a melt-in-the-mouth texture. You can now buy small 500 g (1 lb 2 oz) fish that serve one (it may sound a lot but once the bones and head are gone you end up with about 250 g (9 oz) to eat). Originally it was chicken that was baked in a salt crust until Italian chefs and mammas tried it with fish. It is a very simple cooking method and allows the full flavour of the fish to come through.

serves 4
preparation time: 15 minutes
cooking time: 20–25 minutes

1 x 2 kg (4½ lb) sea bass or 4 x 500 g (1 lb 2 oz) sea bass, gutted and gilled

900 g (2 lb) coarse sea salt

75 g (3 oz) black pepper-corns, lightly crushed

green salad (such as rocket or baby spinach) and lemon wedges, to serve

For the dressing:

175 ml (6 fl oz) extra virgin olive oil

finely grated zest and juice of 1 lemon

6 tablespoons roughly chopped fresh flat-leaf parsley

freshly ground black pepper

1 Pre-heat the oven to 200°C/400°F/Gas Mark 6. Pat the fish dry with kitchen paper. Mix together the sea salt and crushed pepper-corns. Line a large baking tray or roasting tin with foil. Spread a little of the salt mixture on the foil and place the fish on top; if using small fish, arrange them quite close together. Press the remaining salt mixture all over the fish to enclose it completely.

2 Bake the fish for 20–25 minutes, until the salt crust feels hard, is starting to turn golden brown and sounds hollow when tapped. The fish should be hot inside – check by inserting a thin knife. Meanwhile, in a small bowl mix together all the ingredients for the dressing.

3 Once the fish is done, remove it from the oven and immediately scrape away the salt crust and lift off the skin.

4 Gently lift off the flesh with a large palette knife, being careful not to let it touch the salt. Discard all the bones. Put all the fish on a large platter and spoon over some of the dressing. Serve with a light green salad, the remaining dressing and some lemon wedges.

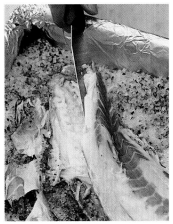

Roast salmon with mostarda di Cremona

Salmon has recently become very popular in Italy. It is easy to cook, since the colour change is so obvious on cooking. Remember, though, that the secret of perfect salmon is to undercook it slightly in the centre so that it remains moist. *Mostarda di Cremona*, or *mostarda di frutta*, is a preserve made of cherries, figs and baby pears in a mustard and honey syrup, readily available in Italian delis and large supermarkets.

serves 4
preparation time: 25 minutes
cooking time: 25 minutes

4 x 200 g (7 oz) pieces of thick salmon fillet

4 tablespoons extra virgin olive oil

juice of ½ lemon

2 tablespoons finely chopped mostarda di Cremona, plus 2 tablespoons syrup from the jar

3 sprigs of fresh mint

450 g (1 lb) new potatoes, preferably Jersey Royals, scrubbed

2 small courgettes, cut into batons

a handful of courgette flowers (optional)

oil for deep frying (optional)

salt and freshly ground black pepper

1 Pre-heat the oven to 200°C/400°F/Gas Mark 6. Rub the salmon with 1 tablespoon of the oil and place in a roasting tin. Sprinkle over the lemon juice and finely chopped mustard fruits and place the mint sprigs on top. Season, then leave to stand at room temperature for 10 minutes.

2 Add the potatoes to a pan of boiling salted water and cook until tender. Meanwhile, roast the salmon for 15 minutes, until just beginning to caramelize on the outside; the inside should still be slightly pink.

3 Bring another pan of water to the boil, add the courgettes and cook for 5 minutes, until just tender. Remove with a slotted spoon and drain. Halve the drained potatoes and mix with the courgettes.

4 Dress the vegetables with the remaining oil and the mustard fruit syrup and season. If using courgette flowers, deep-fry them in hot oil for about 1 minute, until crisp, then drain well. Divide the vegetables between 4 serving plates and top with the salmon fillet, either whole or flaked into large pieces. Garnish with the fried courgette flowers, if using. If liked, serve with extra mustard fruit.

Seared tuna Sicilian style

The first time I managed to feed my daughter, Laura, fresh tuna I had to hide it in a pasta sauce. She loved it so much that now she always asks for fresh tuna and will eat it just grilled with a salad – what a result! Fresh tuna should be served rare or medium rare; if it is cooked all the way through it will become dry.

serves 4
preparation time: 30 minutes
cooking time: 4–10 minutes

1 garlic clove, finely chopped

leaves from 2 sprigs of fresh rosemary, finely chopped

8 fresh sage leaves, finely chopped

1 small red chilli, seeded and finely chopped

50 g (2 oz) fresh white breadcrumbs

finely grated zest of 1 orange

finely grated zest of 1 lemon

4 x 150 g (5 oz) fresh tuna steaks, at least 4 cm (1½ in) thick

2 tablespoons extra virgin olive oil

3 Little Gem lettuces, leaves separated

salt and freshly ground black pepper

For the anchovy dressing:

4 large anchovies packed in salt

1 garlic clove, peeled

2 teaspoons red wine vinegar

120 ml (4 fl oz) extra virgin olive oil

leaves from 2 sprigs of fresh thyme

1 For the dressing, rinse the anchovies under cold water and fillet them, discarding the heads and central bones. Soak the fillets in cold water for 15 minutes, then drain and pat dry on kitchen paper.

2 Using a pestle and mortar, crush the garlic, then add the anchovies, vinegar and half the oil and mix to a paste. Stir in the remaining oil, the thyme leaves and some black pepper.

3 Pre-heat the oven to 200°C/400°F/Gas Mark 6. Mix together the garlic, herbs, chilli, breadcrumbs and citrus zest.

4 Rub the tuna all over with some of the oil, then season with salt and pepper. Coat the fish with the breadcrumb mixture.

5 Heat the remaining oil in a large frying pan and add the tuna. Cook for 1 minute on each side (i.e. 4 minutes in total) to give very rare tuna; for medium rare, transfer the fish to the oven and cook for a further 5 minutes. Leave to stand for 3 minutes. If the fish is thin, it will need only 1–3 minutes' searing in the pan and will not need to go in the oven.

6 Toss the lettuce leaves with some of the anchovy dressing and arrange on 4 serving plates. Slice the tuna and put it on the lettuce. Spoon over any remaining dressing and serve.

Roast cod with caponata

Caponata is a vegetable stew with a characteristic sweet and sour taste that comes from the olives, capers, red wine vinegar and sugar. It tastes just as good cold as hot. Fresh cod is becoming more of a luxury, so when it is available treat it with care. Choose thick, firm fillets from the top end of the fish rather than the tail end and cook for the minimum amount of time to ensure a juicy texture. It's also great fried with chips.

serves 4
preparation time: 30 minutes
cooking time: 45 minutes

2 tablespoons plain flour

4 x 225 g (8 oz) thick cod fillets or steaks

4 tablespoons extra virgin olive oil

4 sprigs of fresh rosemary

For the caponata:

175 ml (6 fl oz) extra virgin olive oil

2 tablespoons plain flour

1 large aubergine, cut into 1 cm (½ in) cubes

2 red onions, finely chopped

2 courgettes, finely diced

2 celery sticks, finely diced

450 g (1 lb) small, ripe plum tomatoes, skinned, seeded and diced

75 g (3 oz) mixed olives, pitted

4 tablespoons capers, rinsed and drained

4 tablespoons red wine vinegar

1 tablespoon soft brown sugar

salt and freshly ground black pepper

1 For the caponata, heat 120 ml (4 fl oz) of the oil in a large ovenproof frying pan. Season the flour with salt and pepper and use to coat the aubergine pieces. Fry the aubergine in the oil for 5–8 minutes, in 2 batches if necessary, until golden brown and tender. Drain on kitchen paper.

2 Wipe clean the frying pan, heat the remaining oil in it and fry the onions for 3 minutes, until just soft. Stir in the courgettes and celery and cook for 5 minutes.

5 Place the fish on top of the caponata and add the rosemary sprigs. Transfer to the oven and roast for 10 minutes, until the fish is tender and milky white all the way through. Drizzle with the remaining oil and serve.

3 Stir in the aubergines, tomatoes, olives, capers, vinegar and sugar and simmer for 10 minutes, until all the vegetables are tender. Season to taste.

4 Pre-heat the oven to 200°C/400°F/Gas Mark 6. To cook the fish, season the flour with salt and pepper, spread it on a plate, then coat the fish in it. Heat half the oil in a large frying pan, add the rosemary sprigs and the fish and cook for 3 minutes on each side, until browned.

Monkfish with tomatoes and herb broth

Monkfish is a firm white fish with a puffy texture. Its flavour is distinctive enough to withstand strong-tasting sauces but in this recipe I like to cook it in a broth with tiny chopped vegetables and herbs so it stays succulent. Serve as a light lunch or, for a more filling meal, put some cooked fettuccine dressed with butter and sage in each serving bowl before adding the fish, vegetables and broth. Try to use good stock here, preferably home-made or bought, organic, fresh vegetable stock.

serves 4
preparation time: 20 minutes
cooking time: 25 minutes

4 tablespoons extra virgin olive oil

1 small red onion, finely diced

1 garlic clove, crushed

1 sprig of fresh rosemary

750 g (1¾ lb) monkfish

1 carrot, finely diced

2 celery sticks, finely diced

350 g (12 oz) baby plum or cherry tomatoes, halved

120 ml (4 fl oz) dry white wine such as Sauvignon Blanc

450 ml (¾ pint) vegetable stock

3 tablespoons fresh thyme leaves

8 fresh sage leaves, finely chopped

sea salt flakes and freshly ground black pepper

1 Pre-heat the oven to 200°C/400°F/Gas Mark 6. Heat half the olive oil in a casserole over a low heat, add the onion, garlic and rosemary and sauté for 5–6 minutes, until soft.

2 Meanwhile, remove the thin membrane from the fish and discard the wings and fins if necessary. Cut out the central bone and cut the fish into 8 pieces. Season with salt and pepper.

3 Add the fish to the pan and cook for 3–4 minutes, turning it several times. Stir in the carrot, celery, tomatoes and wine and simmer for 5 minutes, until the wine has reduced.

4 Add the stock and herbs and bring to the boil, then transfer to the oven and cook for 15 minutes, until the fish is done. Spoon the fish and vegetables into 4 shallow bowls, then gently spoon over the broth. Drizzle over the remaining olive oil and serve.

Chicken saltimbocca

Saltimbocca means 'jump in the mouth' – i.e. the flavours created in the pan are so full of zing that they continue to jump around deliciously once in your mouth! Traditionally, this Roman dish is made with veal. However, chicken breasts are a perfect substitute and will please everyone. Serve with long pasta ribbons and a salad of baby leaves, such as red swiss chard, mizuna and rocket, or simply with courgettes.

serves 4
preparation time: 20 minutes
cooking time: 15–20 minutes

4 x 175 g (6 oz) boneless, skinless chicken breasts

8 thin slices of prosciutto

8 fresh sage leaves

2 tablespoons plain flour

4 tablespoons extra virgin olive oil

25 g (1 oz) butter

100 ml (3½ fl oz) dry white wine

juice of ½ lemon

1 tablespoon finely chopped fresh flat-leaf parsley

sea salt flakes and freshly ground black pepper

1 Open out each chicken breast and place between 2 sheets of clingfilm, then flatten by bashing gently with a rolling pin. Remove the clingfilm and cut each breast in half.

2 Place a slice of prosciutto and a sage leaf on each piece of chicken and secure with a cocktail stick. Season the flour with salt and freshly ground black pepper, then use to coat the chicken breasts.

3 Heat half the oil in a large frying pan and add 4 of the prepared chicken pieces. Cook for 3 minutes on each side, until golden brown. The chicken should be slightly undercooked. Remove and set aside, then cook the remaining chicken in the remaining oil.

4 Clean out the pan and add the butter to it. When it is frothy, add the wine and lemon juice and bring to the boil. Allow to bubble for 1 minute, then return all the chicken to the pan, spooning over the juices, and cook for 2 minutes.

5 Sprinkle the parsley over the top and cook for a further minute. Serve immediately, spooning the juices over the top.

Roast chicken mamma mia style

I named this recipe after my mother because of the influence she had on me when I was growing up and used to cook with her. This chicken dish was one of our favourites and once it was in the oven she would make fresh pasta for the next meal – what a fabulous woman! Ideally this should be served with roast potatoes and spinach. Try and use organic or free-range chicken, which has a much better flavour than battery chickens.

serves 4
preparation time: 20 minutes
cooking time: 50 minutes

leaves from 2 sprigs of fresh rosemary, finely chopped

2 tablespoons chopped fresh thyme

2 garlic cloves, crushed

4 tablespoons extra virgin olive oil

1 x 1.25 kg (2½ lb) chicken, cut into quarters

300 ml (½ pint) dry white wine

sea salt and freshly ground black pepper

1 Pre-heat the oven to 180°C/350°F/Gas Mark 4. Mix the herbs and garlic with 2 tablespoons of the oil and season with salt and pepper.

2 Rub the chicken pieces with the herb mixture, making sure they get a nice even coating.

3 Heat the remaining oil in a large frying pan, add the chicken and fry for 2 minutes on each side, until golden brown. Transfer to a roasting tin.

4 Add the wine to the pan juices and bring to the boil, stirring. Boil for 3 minutes, then pour the wine over the chicken. Roast the chicken for 40 minutes, until cooked through and tender. Serve immediately, with the cooking juices spooned over the top.

Roast chicken with chestnut stuffing

This makes a lovely Sunday lunch or even Christmas dinner. The gravy is quite spectacular and when all the flavours are brought together the dish is very rich, so a little will go a long way. Serve with potatoes and some red cabbage cooked with apples and raisins in balsamic vinegar. What a treat!

In the autumn and winter you could use fresh chestnuts. To prepare them, make a small slit in the skin, then boil for 15 minutes (or roast) and peel off both the hard outer skin and the thin inner skin. Do not use chestnut purée, as this will make the stuffing too thick and stodgy.

> serves 4
> preparation time: 30 minutes
> cooking time: 1¾–2¼ hours

1 x 2 kg (4½ lb) organic or free-range chicken

200 g (7 oz) canned or vacuum-packed whole chestnuts

300 g (11 oz) sausage meat

3 tablespoons chopped mixed fresh herbs, such as flat-leaf parsley, sage and rosemary

6 tablespoons extra virgin olive oil

1 celery stick, cut into 7.5 cm (3 in) lengths

1 carrot, peeled and quartered

1 shallot, peeled and quartered

4 garlic cloves, unpeeled

sea salt flakes and freshly ground black pepper

1 Pre-heat the oven to 160°C/325°F/Gas Mark 3. Remove the band trussing the bird and reserve, then clean the chicken and season it well.

2 Roughly mash the chestnuts with a fork and mix with the sausage meat and herbs. Season well with salt and pepper.

3 Stuff the chicken with the sausage and chestnut mixture and then replace the band to truss it, making sure it is as tight as possible so the stuffing won't fall out.

4 Rub the chicken with 2 tablespoons of oil and then with salt flakes. Put the celery, carrot and shallot in the centre of a large roasting tin to make a bed for the chicken. Put the chicken on top and drizzle with the remaining oil.

5 Roast the chicken for 1¾–2¼ hours, turning it occasionally and adding the garlic cloves about 30 minutes before it is done. To check if the chicken is ready, pierce the breast or the thickest part of the thigh with a fork or skewer; the juices should run clear. Remove the chicken from the tin and set it aside to rest for 10 minutes before carving.

6 To make the gravy, put the vegetables from the roasting tin into a food processor, and add the garlic, squeezed out of its skin. Spoon off and discard about half the fat from the juices in the tin and add to the vegetables and garlic. Blend to a purée, then pass through a sieve, adding a little hot water if the gravy is too thick. Reheat and season if necessary.

7 Remove the stuffing from the chicken and place in a serving bowl. Carve the chicken, starting by removing the drumsticks and thighs. Then carve the white breast meat. Serve with the stuffing and gravy.

Chicken stuffed with bresaola and smoked mozzarella

I tested this recipe on my customers at Zilli Fish and it was a great success. Based on the Seventies classic, chicken Kiev, it has remained the only meat dish on the menu, due to the fact that it is so easy to make. The classic chicken Kiev is deep-fried, but I prefer to brown it in a frying pan and then finish it off in the oven – far healthier. The smoked mozzarella gives it an extra flavour dimension but you could use ordinary mozzarella. It's perfect served with a light salad, pan-fried spinach or pasta dressed with extra virgin olive oil and garlic.

> serves 4
> preparation time: 30 minutes
> cooking time: 30 minutes

4 x 175 g (6 oz) boneless, skinless chicken breasts

150 g (5 oz) smoked mozzarella, peeled and cut into 4 sticks 1 cm (½ in) thick

leaves from 2 sprigs of fresh rosemary, chopped

4 wafer-thin slices of bresaola

2 tablespoons plain flour

1 egg, beaten

4 tablespoons dried bread-crumbs

3 tablespoons extra virgin olive oil

25 g (1 oz) butter

salt and freshly ground black pepper

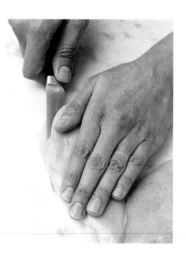
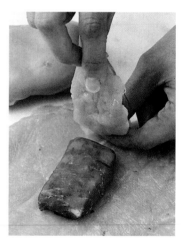

1 Pre-heat the oven to 190°C/375°F/Gas Mark 5. Remove the small inner fillet that lies underneath each chicken breast. Slice the underside of the chicken breast down the centre with a knife, without cutting all the way through, then open it out. Put it between 2 sheets of clingfilm and bash gently with a rolling pin to flatten. Flatten the small fillets, too.

2 Wrap each piece of mozzarella and some chopped rosemary in a slice of bresaola. Take a large chicken breast, smooth-side down, and place a wrapped-up piece of mozza-rella in the centre. Put one of the small fillets on top, folding the remaining chicken over it so the mozzarella parcel is completely enclosed. Turn the chicken over so the join is under-neath. Repeat with the remaining chicken pieces.

3 Season the flour with salt and pepper and spread it over a flat plate. Put the beaten egg on a second plate and the breadcrumbs on a third. Coat the chicken in flour, then egg and finally in the breadcrumbs (it can be chilled at this stage until you are ready to cook it).

4 Heat the olive oil and butter in a large frying pan, add the chicken parcels, seam-side down, and cook for 3 minutes or until golden all over, turning constantly. Transfer to a baking tray and bake for 25–30 minutes, until cooked through. To serve, halve each chicken parcel to reveal the bresaola and melting mozzarella.

Baby chicken diavola

Diavola means devilled, a term used to describe hot dishes. If you are feeding children and think this might be too spicy, you could reduce the amount of chilli. Poussin, baby chicken, spring chicken – they're all the same thing. Allow one per person. You can omit the tomatoes and leave the poussins at room temperature for 30 minutes to absorb the flavours of the rosemary, chilli and garlic, then barbecue them for a tasty summer meal.

serves 4
preparation time: 30 minutes
cooking time: 1 hour

4 x 450 g (1 lb) poussins

2 tablespoons black pepper-corns

2 fresh red chillies, seeded and chopped

leaves from 1 sprig of fresh rosemary

2 garlic cloves, peeled

1 tablespoon coarse sea salt

4 tablespoons extra virgin olive oil

8 plum tomatoes, halved, seeded and roughly chopped

100 ml (3½ fl oz) dry white wine such as Orvieto

 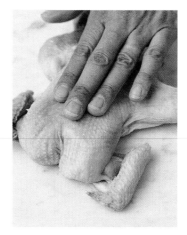 

1 Pre-heat the oven to 220°C/425°F/Gas Mark 7. Remove and discard the elastic holding each poussin, then turn the poussin over so it is breast-side down. Cut along one side of the back-bone with a pair of strong kitchen scissors to open out the bird.

2 Cut along the other side of the backbone and remove it to neaten that edge. Open out the bird, turn it breast-side up, and press down on it with the palm of your hand to flatten it. This process is known as spatchcocking. Wash the birds and pat them dry on kitchen paper.

3 Crush the peppercorns with a pestle and mortar (or in a small bowl with the end of a rolling pin). Add the chillies, rosemary leaves, garlic and sea salt and crush again with the peppercorns. Rub this mixture all over the poussins.

4 Take a roasting tin large enough to hold the poussins and place on the hob. Heat the oil in it, then add the poussins, skin-side down, and cook for about 5 minutes, until golden brown and crisp. Turn over and cook for a further 3 minutes.

5 Sprinkle the tomatoes over the birds and add the wine. Bring to the boil, then transfer the roasting tin to the oven and bake for 50 minutes, until the birds are crisp and cooked through and the tomatoes have just started to char in places. Serve the poussins whole or cut into pieces, with a rocket and Parmesan salad.

Grilled rump steak paillard

This simple way of cooking steak is very popular in Italy. You could serve this dish with the best roast potatoes – parboil them and coat them in semolina, then roast with olive oil, garlic and rosemary for 15 minutes – yummy! How you grill your steaks and radicchio is up to you but make sure the grill is very hot.

serves 4
preparation time: 10 minutes
cooking time: 10 minutes

2 heads of Treviso radicchio

5 tablespoons extra virgin olive oil

2 lemons

4 x 200 g (7 oz) rump steaks

1 tablespoon chopped fresh flat-leaf parsley

sea salt flakes and freshly ground black pepper

  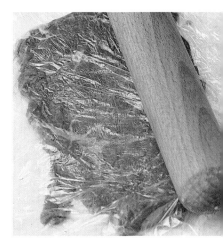

1 Pre-heat a ridged chargrill pan until smoking. Cut each head of radicchio into 4 wedges. Drizzle over 2 tablespoons of the olive oil and the juice of half a lemon.

2 Griddle the radicchio for 2 minutes on each side, then remove and drizzle over another tablespoon of olive oil. Keep warm. Cut the remaining whole lemon into quarters and griddle for 1 minute on each side. Set aside.

3 Put each steak between 2 sheets of clingfilm and bash with a rolling pin or meat mallet until very flat. Season the steaks and rub with a tiny bit of the remaining oil.

4 Griddle the steaks for 1 minute on each side, then remove from the grill pan and roll them up.

5 Mix together the remaining olive oil, the juice from the remaining lemon half and the parsley. Put the steaks in the centre of 4 warmed serving plates with 2 wedges of radicchio and spoon over some of the dressing. Drizzle the remaining dressing around the steaks and serve with the grilled lemon.

Roasted lamb fillets with Italian gravy

Make sure you buy either best end or loin of lamb fillets, as these are very tender. On St Patrick's Day one year I was in Dublin cooking for Chris Evans' breakfast show team and I overslept! This was a major problem, as I was supposed to make an Irish stew. When I found this cut of meat in the fridge I was incredibly relieved, as it took me only 30 minutes to make a really tender Irish stew – with an Italian feel, of course! Any other cut of meat would have taken up to an hour. Serve this with Parmesan mash and some buttered spinach in garlic and olive oil.

> serves 4
> preparation time: 20 minutes
> cooking time: 25 minutes

200 g (7 oz) thinly sliced pancetta or smoked bacon (about 12 slices)

4 small sprigs of fresh rosemary

4 x 175 g (6 oz) best end or loin of lamb fillets

2 tablespoons olive oil

2 celery sticks, roughly chopped

2 carrots, roughly chopped

1 shallot, halved

2 garlic cloves, crushed

1 small red chilli, seeded and chopped

120 ml (4 fl oz) red wine

450 ml (¾ pint) meat stock

1 teaspoon plain flour, mixed to a paste with 1 teaspoon soft butter

salt and freshly ground black pepper

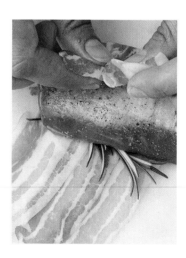

1 Pre-heat the oven to 220°C/425°F/Gas Mark 7. Lay out the pancetta or smoked bacon on a board in groups of 3 strips at a 40-degree angle. Place a sprig of rosemary in the centre of each. Season the lamb fillets, then put them on top of the rosemary and tightly roll the pancetta around the meat.

2 Heat the oil in a large oven-proof frying pan, add the vegetables, garlic and chilli and sauté for 5 minutes, stirring regularly. Move the vegetables to one side of the pan and add the meat parcels, seam-side down. Cook over a high heat for 2 minutes, until browned all over, finishing seam-side down again.

5 Return the gravy to the pan over a low heat and whisk in the butter and flour mixture, stirring constantly. Boil for 1 minute, until slightly thickened. Serve the lamb with the Italian gravy.

3 Pour the wine over the meat, bring to the boil and simmer for 2 minutes. Add the stock and bring to the boil. Transfer the pan to the oven and cook for 12–15 minutes, until the lamb is tender but still pink in the centre.

4 Take the lamb out of the pan and keep warm. To make the gravy, put the vegetables and juices from the pan into a food processor and blend until smooth, then pass through a sieve.

Sausage and borlotti casserole

This is a lovely winter warmer, especially for large families. My mother had to feed eight children, so she created this inexpensive dish. She served it with polenta, a delicious combination.

serves 4

preparation time: 35 minutes

cooking time: 50 minutes

3 tablespoons olive oil

8 Italian sausages

1 onion, chopped

2 garlic cloves, chopped

450 g (1 lb) carrots diced

1 celery heart, diced

2 leeks, finely chopped

200 ml (7 fl oz) dry white wine such as Sauvignon Blanc

150 ml (¼ pint) stock

1 cooking apple, peeled, cored and finely chopped

1 bay leaf

400 g (14 oz) can of borlotti beans, drained and rinsed

1 teaspoon plain flour, mixed to a paste with 1 teaspoon soft butter (optional)

salt and freshly ground black pepper

For the wet polenta:

1 litre (1¾ pints) water

2 teaspoons salt

175 g (6 oz) polenta flour

50 g (2 oz) butter

100 g (4 oz) Parmesan cheese, freshly grated

3 tablespoons chopped fresh flat-leaf parsley, extra for garnish

1 Heat the oil in a large, deep pan. Add the sausages, onion, garlic, carrots, celery and leeks, stir well and cook for 10 minutes, until just turning golden brown.

2 Add the wine, stock, apple, bay leaf and some salt and pepper. Bring to the boil, then reduce the heat and simmer for 30 minutes, until the sausages are cooked through and the vegetables are tender.

3 Stir in the borlotti beans and cook for 10 minutes. If the juices need to be thickened slightly, add the flour paste, stirring constantly, and cook for 1 minute.

4 To make the polenta, bring the water to the boil in a large, deep pan with the salt. Reduce the heat and gradually add the polenta, stirring constantly with a whisk. Simmer for 20 minutes, until the polenta is very thick and is coming away from the side of the pan; it may seem the polenta has thickened faster than this but it really must cook on to allow the grains to become tender.

5 Beat the butter and Parmesan into the polenta and season to taste, adding plenty of freshly ground black pepper. Stir in the parsley. To serve, divide the polenta between 4 large, shallow bowls and spoon over the sausage and vegetable mixture, then spoon over the juices.

Calf's liver Veneziana

Calf's liver has a light flavour compared to other offal. When cooked correctly, it melts in the mouth. For maximum flavour it is important to sear liver over a high heat and keep the centre just pink. Overcooked liver turns grainy, tough and grey. Do not be tempted to wash liver as this makes it discolour on cooking. It's very good served with buttery mash or creamy polenta. This recipe is an old favourite of mine and it is still on my menu today.

serves 4
preparation time: 20 minutes
cooking time: 20 minutes

2 tablespoons extra virgin olive oil

40 g (1½ oz) butter

450 g (1 lb) red onions, thinly sliced

450 g (1 lb) calf's liver, thinly sliced

2 tablespoons plain flour

6 sage leaves

4 tablespoons Marsala wine

2 tablespoons red wine

2 tablespoons chopped fresh parsley

salt and freshly ground black pepper

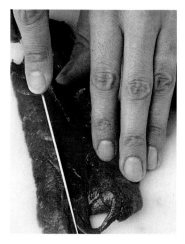

1 Heat the oil and half the butter in a large frying pan. Add the onions and cook over a low heat for 15 minutes, until they become very soft and translucent.

2 Meanwhile, pat the liver dry on kitchen paper and then cut it into strips 1 cm (½ in) wide. Put the flour on a large plate and season with salt and pepper. Coat the liver in the seasoned flour.

3 Remove the onions from the pan with a slotted spoon and keep warm. Raise the heat and add the liver and sage leaves to the pan. Cook over a high heat for 2 minutes, until browned.

5 Return the onions to the pan, then stir in the remaining butter and the parsley. Cook for 2 minutes and serve immediately.

4 Add the Marsala and red wine to the pan and cook for 2 minutes, until slightly reduced.

DESSERTS

Traditional zabaglione

When I was a child, my mother used to make cold zabaglione for breakfast. It gave us a great boost to get through our lessons at school. I recommend Savoiardi biscuits to dip in the zabaglione, but any sweet biscuits will do; my daughter, Laura, loves it with chocolate biscuits.

serves 6
preparation time: 10 minutes
cooking time: 10 minutes

5 egg yolks

1 egg

6 tablespoons caster sugar

8 tablespoons Marsala

100 g (4 oz) strawberries, hulled and sliced, plus 6 small whole ones

12–18 Savoiardi, cantucci or amaretti biscuits, to serve

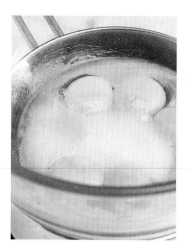

1 Put the egg yolks, whole egg and sugar in a large heatproof bowl and set it over a pan of barely simmering water.

2 Using a handheld electric beater, whisk the mixture until it first becomes a light froth and then changes to a thick, mousse-like consistency. This should take about 5 minutes with an electric beater (you could use a balloon whisk but it will take twice as long).

3 Drizzle in spoonfuls of the Marsala, whisking all the time. Remove the bowl from the pan of water and continue to whisk, first for 1 minute on high, then 2 minutes on medium and finally 4–5 minutes on slow. The mixture will thicken even more and hold its shape, while becoming lighter and smoother.

4 Divide the strawberries between 6 tall serving glasses and spoon in the warm zabaglione and garnish with the whole strawberries. Serve warm, with a few biscuits on the side.

Ricotta and Amarena cherry tart

Amarena cherries are wild cherries from Bologna, available in jars from some delicatessens and supermarkets. They make a lovely instant sauce for ice cream, or you can use them in this tart to make a stunning dessert for a dinner party or summer tea party.

serves 8
preparation time: 40 minutes, plus 30 minutes' chilling
cooking time: 25 minutes

250 g (9 oz) ricotta cheese

3 tablespoons icing sugar, sifted

4–6 tablespoons Amaretto liqueur, to taste

300 ml (½ pint) double cream

600 g (1 lb 5 oz) jar of Amarena Fabbri wild cherries in syrup

25 g (1 oz) flaked almonds, toasted

For the pastry:

175 g (6 oz) plain flour

2 tablespoons caster sugar

100 g (4 oz) chilled butter, cut into cubes

2 egg yolks

2 tablespoons cold water

1 First make the pastry: sift the flour into a large bowl and stir in the sugar. Rub in the butter with your fingertips until the mixture resembles fine breadcrumbs.

2 Add the egg yolks and water and stir with a fork until the mixture forms large clumps. Bring it together with your hands to make a dough. Knead gently on a lightly floured surface until smooth, then wrap in clingfilm and chill for 20 minutes.

3 Pre-heat the oven to 200°C/400°F/Gas Mark 6. Roll out the pastry on a lightly floured surface and use to line a 20 cm (8 in) loose-based tart tin. Trim the edge and prick the base with a fork. Chill for 10 minutes.

4 Line the pastry case with baking parchment and fill with baking beans, then bake blind for 15 minutes. Remove the beans and paper and bake for a further 10 minutes, until crisp and golden. Leave on a wire rack to cool.

5 Meanwhile, make the filling: put the ricotta in a bowl with the icing sugar and Amaretto liqueur and beat until smooth. In a separate bowl, whisk the cream until it forms soft peaks. Fold the cream into the ricotta mixture.

6 Drain the cherries, reserving the syrup. Spoon the ricotta filling into the pastry case and level the surface. Spoon the drained cherries over the top and fill the gaps with the flaked almonds.

7 Chill the tart until required.
Just before serving, spoon
3–4 tablespoons of the
reserved cherry syrup over
the tart. Slice and serve with
extra syrup.

Pannacotta with fresh berries

Pannacotta means 'cooked cream' and it makes a simple but luxurious dessert. It is best made with a vanilla pod rather than vanilla extract, as the seeds that fall into the cream mixture give it a fresh vanilla flavour and speckled appearance. Don't throw vanilla pods away after use; simply rinse them if necessary, then dry and place in a pot of sugar. A couple of days later you will have vanilla sugar, perfect for sprinkling over fresh fruit.

serves 4
preparation time: 20 minutes, plus 3 hours' chilling
cooking time: 10 minutes

4 tablespoons caster sugar

300 ml (½ pint) double cream

300 ml (½ pint) milk

1 vanilla pod, split open lengthways

175 g (6 oz) mascarpone cheese

2 tablespoons Marsala

2 level teaspoons gelatine granules

For the berries:

100 g (4 oz) caster sugar

50 ml (2 fl oz) water

finely grated zest of 1 lime

juice of ½ lime

2 sprigs of fresh mint

50 g (2 oz) each of black-berries, strawberries and blueberries (slice or halve the blackberries and strawberries if large)

1 Put the sugar, cream, milk and vanilla pod in a pan, bring to the boil and simmer for 5–8 minutes, stirring occasionally. Remove the pan from the heat and take out the vanilla pod. Whisk the mascarpone into the hot cream mixture.

2 Put the Marsala in a small bowl and sprinkle over the gelatine. Leave it to swell for 5 minutes, then place the bowl over a small pan of simmering water, making sure the water does not touch the base of the bowl, and leave until the gelatine has completely dissolved. Stir it into the warm cream.

3 Lightly oil four 200 ml (7 fl oz) ramekins or glass pots and pour in the cream mixture. Chill for 3 hours or overnight, until set (it will keep for 3–4 days in the fridge).

4 To make the berry compote; put the sugar and water in a small pan and heat gently until the sugar has dissolved, then boil for 1 minute. Leave the syrup to cool for 5 minutes, then add the lime zest and juice, mint sprigs and fruit. Leave to cool completely.

5 To serve, turn out the pannacotta: dip each ramekin in a bowl of hot water for 30 seconds and then invert on to a serving plate or bowl, giving it a good shake to release. Discard the mint sprigs from the compote, then spoon the fruits and syrup around the pannacotta.

Tiramisu

I can say little about this famous dessert other than recommend you use the right biscuits. In Italy tiramisu is made with Pavesini biscuits, which are smaller and lighter than Savoiardi. Available in Italian delis, they give this rich dessert a lovely light texture.

serves 8–10

preparation time: 30 minutes

4 egg yolks

150 g (5 oz) caster sugar

250 g (9 oz) mascarpone cheese

300 ml (½ pint) double cream

2 tablespoons dry Marsala

2 tablespoons Tia Maria

2 teaspoons vanilla extract

300–450 ml (½–¾ pint) strong espresso coffee (the amount you need will depend on which biscuits you use), at room temperature

60 Pavesini or 30 Savoiardi biscuits

3 tablespoons unsweetened cocoa powder

50 g (2 oz) dark chocolate shavings

This recipe contains raw eggs and is not suitable for pregnant women.

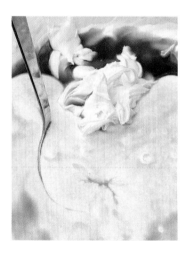
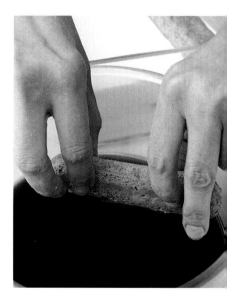

1 Put the egg yolks and sugar in a large bowl and whisk for about 5 minutes with an electric beater until the mixture is thick and mousse-like (if you use a balloon whisk it will take 5–10 minutes longer).

2 In a separate bowl, beat the mascarpone and cream together until thick, then gradually fold in the Marsala, Tia Maria, vanilla extract, and egg and sugar mixture until smooth and thoroughly combined.

3 Take a 20 x 30 cm (8 x 12 in) dish about 7.5 cm (3 in) deep and spread a third of the cream mixture over the base. Put the espresso in a shallow bowl and lightly soak each biscuit in it one by one before arranging them in a layer on top of the cream. Cover with a second layer of the cream.

4 Continue like this to the top, ending with a layer of biscuits (it should be the third layer). Tap the dish to settle the contents, then sift over the cocoa powder and dust with chocolate shavings. Chill for 1–2 hours, although it should be firm enough to cut into squares after 30 minutes.

If you prefer, you could serve Tiramisu in individual serving bowls like this glass one.

Pine nut semifreddo

The translation of semifreddo is quite simply 'half cold', meaning it is not quite ice cream. However, it is a very good replacement. The wonderful thing is you don't need any fancy equipment to make it and it is fantastic for a dinner party, as it can be made in advance and then forgotten about. So go for it and enjoy yourself.

serves 8
preparation time: 30 minutes,
   plus about 3 hours' freezing
cooking time: 8 minutes

Praline, a mixture of nuts and sugar, is very easy to make and, once crushed, can be frozen and used straight from the freezer. Here I've used pine nuts since they are so Italian, but feel free to use almonds, hazelnuts or pistachios if you prefer.
A delicious accompaniment to this dessert is roasted fruits, such as plums, cherries or peaches. Just sprinkle them with vanilla sugar (see page 114) and a splash of red wine or Marsala and roast in a hot oven for 15 minutes, until tender and juicy. Serve warm or cold.

1 vanilla pod

4 eggs, separated

4 tablespoons caster sugar

300 ml (½ pint) double or
   whipping cream

a pinch of salt

For the praline:

150 g (5 oz) pine nuts

200 g (7 oz) caster sugar

4 tablespoons water

1 First make the praline. Pre-heat the oven to 180°C/350°F/Gas Mark 4. Spread the pine nuts out on a baking sheet and toast in the oven for 8 minutes or until golden (make sure you keep a close eye on them because if you overcook them they will become really bitter). Remove from the oven and leave to cool.

2 Put the sugar and water into a heavy-based saucepan and place over a medium-high heat. The mixture will first start bubbling, then become a clear syrup and then start to turn golden in parts. Carefully shake the pan to mix in the coloured parts.

4 As soon as the caramel becomes dark golden, remove from the heat and pour it on to a lightly oiled baking tray – take great care as it will be dangerously hot. Leave until cold and set. Break up the praline. Put half of it in a food processor and pulse until quite fine, then set aside. Put the remaining praline in the food processor and pulse until more finely crushed but not powdery.

3 When the syrup has become a golden brown caramel, tip the pan away from you and carefully pour in the pine nuts. Turn the heat down to a simmer and gently stir the nuts to coat them in the caramel.

5 To make the semifreddo mixture, halve the vanilla pod lengthways, scrape out the seeds with a teaspoon and put them in a bowl with the egg yolks and sugar. Whisk until the mixture turns pale.

6 In another bowl, whisk the cream to soft peaks. Then, in a third bowl, using a clean whisk, whisk the egg whites with a pinch of salt until they form stiff peaks.

7 Fold the cream into the egg yolk mixture, then fold in the egg whites. Finally fold in the finely crushed praline. Pour the mixture into a freezer-proof container and freeze for 3 hours, until firm. Serve in scoops, with the remaining praline.

Menus

On a recent trip to Italy I noticed that the old Italian restaurants have moved on from heavy, oily sauces and that nobody seems to have more than two courses any more, with one of these being pasta. So gone are the days of *antipasti, primi, secondi* and *dessert*. The more healthy diet is definitely popular, and includes grilled fish or meat, simple salads, and pasta with light sauces. Using my book you should have a good guide to help you keep that great figure.

In the old way of Italian eating you always sat at the table, where you found lots of different *antipasti* with nice crusty breads, a good bottle of extra virgin olive oil and a variety of cheeses. Italians are very bad at waiting for food, and maybe this was why when you sat at the table the food was already there. Meanwhile, the pasta could be put on (this course is called the *primi piatti*), and was traditionally mixed with a sauce prepared earlier in the day.

Then after the pasta you would have the *secondo piatto con verdure* (the main course), which is fish or meat with salad, green vegetables and some potatoes.

Il dessert might be *gelato* (ice-cream) or *frutta di stagione* (seasonal fruit). Then, of course, you would go to the local bar for a great *espresso con Amaro* as a digestif. Now let me take you through a few of my ideas for entertaining the Italian way. You should increase or decrease the quantities for some of the dishes in the menus below, to serve the required number of people, but most of the recipes are very easygoing and adaptable so this shouldn't be a problem. Don't forget that these menus are just a guideline. If they contain something you don't like or haven't got, try something else, and have a great time in your kitchen.

Arrivederci e buona fortuna!

Dinner Party for 6

Six is just the right number for a dinner party. But make sure you are well prepared, as you don't want to end up spending most of your time in the kitchen. The polenta can be made in advance and so can the dessert.

Polenta with Wild and Field Mushrooms

Roasted Lamb Fillets with Italian Gravy

Ricotta and Amarena Cherry Tart

Buffet for 20 People

In the summer months Italian food really comes into its own. This is when you cook outdoors and have either a hot or cold buffet or even a barbecue. Some of the recipes in this book are very appropriate for this type of entertaining. The sea bass, for example, is great, as it will keep warm in its crust for a long time after cooking.

Tiger Prawns on Skewers

Buffalo Mozzarella and Rocket with Roasted Red Pepper Salsa

A large tray of Rigatoni with Traditional Pork Bolognese

Grilled Field Mushrooms with Dolcelatte

Roast Salmon with mostarda di Cremona (either whole or fillets)

Sea Bass with a Sea Salt and Black Pepper Crust

Fennel, Radicchio and Gorgonzola Salad

Chicken Mamma Mia Style

Large tray of Tiramisu and lots of fresh fruit

Simple Dinner Party for 6

This menu is very straightforward. You can roast the vegetables for the starter well in advance, then just put the cheese on top and grill at the last minute … easy.

Roasted Vegetables with Goat's Cheese and Basil Oil

Roast Chicken Mamma Mia Style

Tiramisu

Family Meal for 4

Often in my house not everybody likes the same food, so I try to stick to very simple recipes. My daughter Laura and I love Gnocchi with Pesto, so we make it together all the time and we usually have it as a main meal with a nice salad. Here is an example of a typical evening in my household.

Minestrone of Rice and Vegetables

Gnocchi with Pesto and Green Beans

Buffalo Mozzarella and Rocket with Roasted Red Peppers

Zabaglione with fresh strawberries (if in season)

Vegetarian Dinner for 6

Italian food lends itself to vegetarianism because pasta can be a very good, filling meal with just a simple tomato sauce. But there are plenty of other interesting choices in this book. The Pine Nut Semifreddo is a great dessert as you can make it the day before.

Roasted Stuffed Onions

Radicchio and Fennel Risotto

or Angel Hair Pasta with Vegetables and Smoked Mozzarella

Pine Nut Semifreddo

Romantic Dinner for 2

Valentine's Day is approaching, you forget to make a booking in a restaurant and you have to compromise by cooking for your partner. Now, you want to have plenty of time for drinking a glass of champagne before dinner. So stick to a very simple starter, like the asparagus I have chosen here, which is also an aphrodisiac (very good), and you can wrap it and leave it on a grill tray until you are ready to sit down. Then you just grill it for a few minutes and serve on hot plates with a nice glass of Prosecco. Another good choice for a main course is the sea bass, although it is a little messy. Your dessert also needs to be prepared beforehand so it gives you time to spend with your partner.

Asparagus and Parma Ham Gratin

Roast Cod with Caponata

Pannacotta with Fresh Berries

Index

Where to buy good Italian food

Italian ingredients are now very easy to buy in supermarkets. However, a trip to a good delicatessen fills you with inspiration and ideas. Many are starting to stock organic produce, too. Here is just a handful of good food shops and delis that stock excellent olive oils, balsamic vinegar, cheeses, pasta, cured meats, Italian wines and some fresh herbs and vegetables.

Atlas Delicatessen

345 Deansgate, Manchester M3 4LY
Tel: 0161 834 2266
As the name implies, this deli has produce from all over the world, including China and Japan. It is well known for local cheeses and cakes.

Camisa

61 Old Compton Street, London W1V 5PN
Tel: 020 7437 7610
Stocks every dried pasta you can think of, best-ever fresh ravioli, good cheeses, cured meats and sausages. Plus some classic Italian wines.

Lina Stores

18 Brewer Street, London W1R 3FS
Tel: 020 7437 6482
Brilliant Italian deli stocking beautiful fresh pasta, pesto, Italian sausages, Pavesini biscuits, salted anchovies, Amarena cherries, fresh herbs, *del verde* dry pasta and breads. Mail order available.

St James Delicatessen

9–11 St James Street, Derby DE1 1QT
Tel: 0133 233 1255
Stocks fresh seasonal porcini and a vast range of antipasti.

Silver Palate

3 Vaughan Road, Harpenden, Herts AL5 4HU
Tel: 0158 271 3722
e-mail: info@silverpalate.co.uk
A Mediterranean deli, specializing in olives. Stocks all Italian classics, plus a few more from surrounding Mediterranean countries. Mail order available.

Tom's Deli

226 Westbourne Grove, London W11 2RH
Tel: 020 7221 8818
e-mail: tomsdeli@easynet.co.uk
Excellent fresh breads, freshly made pesto, salads and anchovies. Mail order available.

Valvona and Crolla

19 Elm Row, Edinburgh EH7 4AA
Tel: 0131 556 6066
www.valvonacrolla.co.uk
e-mail: sales@valvonacrolla.co.uk
This famous Edinburgh deli has been in the Contini family since 1934. Mail order available.

Villandry

170 Great Portland Street, London W1N 5TB
Tel: 020 7631 3131
As well as Italian foods, Villandry stocks excellent fresh Mediterranean fruit and vegetables, including many organic ones. Fabulous fresh breads, cheeses and cured meats. Mail order available.

Finally, two brilliant foodstores in London are Planet Organic (tel: 020 7221 7171 for details) and Fresh and Wild (tel: 020 7428 7575). They both stock a wide range of organic food, including wonderful fruit, vegetables and herbs. For the best olives available, go to Saponara in Islington (tel: 020 7226 2771).